Praise for *Cracking Health Costs*

"In their new book, *Cracking Health Costs*, Tom Emerick and Al Lewis manage to gore everyone's ox in such a delightful way that you will laugh out loud even while you are cringing at some of the ways you too have fallen into the traps they so vividly describe. They blow up myths about the benefits of wellness, prevention, screening, PBMs, and much more. And they name names and provide links and references to support their suppositions, and, most important, they do the math. Even if you don't agree with everything they posit, you will want to read this book at least a couple of times not only to mine the nuggets, but also to enjoy the humor."

—**Patricia Salber**, MD, MBA,
Host, *The Doctor Weighs In* and
CEO of Health Tech Hatch

"Tom Emerick is one of the nation's most experienced and successful benefits managers. He is offering guideposts to avoiding overpricing and overtreatment in health plans. The need for such guideposts is a reproach to the American healthcare system. Nonetheless, the insights are profound for benefits managers and beneficial for employees."

—**Nortin M. Hadler**, MD, MACP, MACR, FACOEM,
Professor of Medicine and Microbiology/Immunology,
University of North Carolina at Chapel Hill

"*Cracking Health Costs* is a myth-shattering book that opens Pandora's box! While many administrators, patients, and healthcare workers are caught in the cultural web of unnecessary procedures, accidents, waste, and poor quality, Emerick and Lewis empower health benefits managers to call the shots by debunking common myths and illuminating a clear, practical road map for change. Knowledge is power, and power is within these pages. This book will transform healthcare."

—**Kathleen Bartholomew**, RN, MN,
Author and Nurse Leader

"*Cracking Health Costs* debunks the fads in corporate health benefit management and provides a road map for executives who want their employees to have top-quality care at an affordable price."

—**Rosemary Gibson**, Author of *The Treatment Trap:
How the Overuse of Medical Care Is Wrecking Your Health
and What You Can Do to Prevent It*

"The overuse, underuse, and misuse of healthcare services fueled by decades of blind purchasing has created the single most important threat to the health and wealth of our families. When in a crisis, it is critical to take a hard look at the facts no matter how painful it is. This book is a courageous and inspired work that is a must read for our nation's corporate and healthcare leaders who must get out of the stands and wade into the arena as Tom Emerick has . . . this is a David and Goliath story. Our fight with the status quo is one our nation can't afford to lose."

—Charles R. Denham, MD,
Chairman TMIT,
CEO HCC Corporation

"Tom Emerick and co-author Al Lewis have crafted a work that should, and hopefully will, become required reading in America's boardrooms and executive suites, as well as the dysfunctional mess we refer to as Congress. Tom's pedigree alone is worthy of serious national attention. As benefits manager for healthcare for over a million employees he guided Walmart to a Renaissance in approaching the responsibilities of providing quality and safe healthcare versus just writing the checks, and his experiences alone would justify reading this work. But *Cracking Health Costs* is far more: a very straightforward and readable story of how we can transform ourselves from victims of a collapsing financial model of healthcare into leaders of a revolution in smart choices and careful selection of who gets our dollars."

—John J. Nance, Author of *Why Hospitals Should Fly* and *Charting the Course*

"This book is a roadmap for how some private equity companies already spend their money wisely on health benefits in their portfolio companies, rather than chase every fad that, as Emerick and Lewis point out, can and do harm your employees as well as your bottom line."

—Tom Scully, Administrator, Centers for Medicare and Medicaid Services (2001–2003); Senior Counsel, Alston & Bird; Partner, Welsh Carson, Anderson & Stowe

CRACKING HEALTH COSTS

CRACKING

HOW TO CUT YOUR COMPANY'S COSTS

HEALTH

AND PROVIDE EMPLOYEES BETTER CARE

COSTS

TOM EMERICK
AL LEWIS

WILEY

Cover image: © iStockphoto.com/Health Care Costs
Cover design: C. Wallace

For general information about our other products and services, please contact our Customer Care Department within the United States at (800) 762-2974, outside the United States at (317) 572-3993 or fax (317) 572-4002.

Wiley publishes in a variety of print and electronic formats and by print-on-demand. Some material included with standard print versions of this book may not be included in e-books or in print-on-demand. If this book refers to media such as a CD or DVD that is not included in the version you purchased, you may download this material at http://booksupport.wiley.com. For more information about Wiley products, visit www.wiley.com.

Library of Congress Cataloging-in-Publication Data:
Emerick, Tom, 1947-
    Cracking health costs: how to cut your company's costs and provide employees better care / Tom Emerick and Al Lewis.
        pages cm
    Includes bibliographical references.
    ISBN 978-1-118-63648-0 (cloth); ISBN 978-1-118-71123-1 (ebk); ISBN 978-1-118-71091-3 (ebk)
    1.   Health insurance—United States–Costs. 2.   Health insurance–United States–Cost control. 3.   Employees–Medical care–United States–Cost control. I.   Lewis, Alfred. II.   Title.
    HG9396.E44 2013
    658.3'254–dc23   2013012719

Printed in the United States of America

10   9   8   7   6   5   4   3   2   1

Contents

Foreword

If you run an organization, work in human resources (HR), employ people, or have responsibility for your company's income statement, you are probably more concerned about controlling your organization's health insurance costs than about global warming, government debt, or al Qaeda. After all, health insurance benefits may be either the second or the third most expensive item on your income statement (second after labor costs in service industries, third in manufacturing after labor and cost of goods). In the past, most HR professionals/CEOs/CFOs paid little attention to trying to manage this expense—that was the work of the insurance companies, managed care organizations, providers, vendors, and consultants hired to design, manage, and perform oversight of this area. Well, if you think the carriers, providers, vendors, government, or consultants will (or can) fix your problem, I have a bridge to sell you.

Fixing healthcare costs should be one of the top priorities for every employer, for not only competitiveness but, for many, survival. As a healthcare consultant, I meet daily with C-suites telling me their margins can't absorb double-digit benefit costs increases and survive. Most have pushed cost shifting to employees to the limit—so now they have fretfully grasped at population health management (PHM) as the next silver bullet. Seventy-five percent have wellness programs, 15 percent of large employers mandate health risk assessments and biometrics for insurance eligibility, and 30 percent are considering on-site clinics—but do these things really work? Few employers have a three- to five-year strategic plan for health risk mitigation or understand the strategies that do work. Fewer still know how to measure their PHM strategies' success or failure.

As someone who heads a department responsible for the data analytics and population health enhancement strategies for our clients, I readily admit I've made many of the mistakes pointed out in *Cracking Health Costs*. We learn from our mistakes. As a benefit consultant, a physician, and an ex–managed care insurance executive, I've sat on just about every side of the PHM fence. Today it is no longer about wellness programs, health reimbursement accounts (HRAs), biometrics, or paying people to engage. Sure, those have their place, but don't rely on them as your strategy. I couldn't get my patients to lose weight, stop abusing alcohol and tobacco, or exercise when I was a practicing physician. Why did I think, as a benefit consultant, I could influence employee health any better? People abuse substances, are couch potatoes, or are overnutritionalized (that's HR-speak for "fat") because they hate their jobs, live in a grocery desert, have a failed marriage, have kids who are on drugs, are poor, or have bad genes, or they just don't care. Only 1 percent of the U.S. population exercises 150 minutes a week, sleeps seven to eight hours a night, eats five to nine fruits and vegetables a day, and doesn't abuse alcohol or use tobacco products. I give employers the same message I used to give my patients: "Well-being is the opposite of dis-ease. A well-lived life is like a four-legged stool. The legs are physical, mental, socioeconomic, and spiritual well-being. All four legs must be present and in balance for a person to be at-ease, not dis-eased." If your HR department is ready to undertake the root causes of what is really driving your plan costs (that includes spouses and dependents, who represent 50 to 60 percent of your direct medical costs), then you will start focusing on their well-being, not just their biometrics. This is not easy stuff; this is hard work. You need to learn from others' mistakes and conserve your resources, focusing on what works.

In *Cracking Health Costs*, Tom Emerick and Al Lewis break down many of the myths around population health management. There is no silver bullet. Well-being means focusing on the work environment, making the workplace somewhere people want to go every morning. What if every employee woke up each Monday morning like Sam Walton did and said, "Thank God, it's Monday!"? Nobody had to pay Sam an incentive to go to work.

As a physician and a benefit consultant, I know that too much healthcare can kill you. Maybe you didn't read the 1999 Institute of Medicine's report, *To Err Is Human*, telling us that as many as 98,000 people die each year in hospitals due to medical errors, but you should know what *your* procedural complication events per thousand rate is—a category in most medical claim reviews that can be accessed by your carrier or healthcare adviser. Who are the providers with high compli-cation rates? Is your pharmacy benefit management (PBM) drug mix maximizing your actual savings or just your PBM rebates? Do you understand why executive physicals, prostate-specific antigen (PSA) testing, yearly paps and mammograms, and annual physicals are a waste of money? Are you still trying to bribe your plan members into living a healthier lifestyle with cash incentives? Did that work with your kids? If so, for how long? Incentives might drive engagement, but not commitment.

Cracking Health Costs addresses all of these issues and is a must-read for any corporate executive who believes that having healthier, happier, more productive employees should be a business strategy, as opposed to a button that can be pushed with vendors, bribes, and surveys. Tom Emerick faced these same challenges at Burger King, British Petroleum, and lastly with Walmart as Vice President, Global Benefit Design. Al Lewis is the preeminent population health manage-ment measurement guru and return on investment (ROI) myth buster. Tom and Al have written a fascinating book outlining many of the wasteful strategies currently being adopted by corporate America, and suggesting better ways to attack this problem.

—David A. Rearick, DO, MBA, CPE, Chief Medical Officer,
Marsh & McLennan Agency Mid-Atlantic Region

Introduction

Warning: Healthcare can be hazardous to your company's physical and financial health.

This book is about fixing both those hazards, through less and smarter utilization of your healthcare benefit. Specifically, we will propose that you reduce your company's healthcare spending by spending less money on your company's healthcare. I know it sounds like a Yogi Berra quote, and you may be wondering why you just paid for a book that states something that obvious, but the fact is, just about every solution that you are pitched by your carriers, vendors, and consultants urges you to spend money now for the promise of a return on investment later.

Unfortunately, for reasons detailed in *Cracking Health Costs'* prequel, *Why Nobody Believes the Numbers*, most of those ROIs are rather transparently (and in many cases, hilariously) made up. Don't take my word for it. Look at your own spending patterns. As you can tell by from your own utilization rates for scans, prescriptions, lab tests, and primary care—not to mention your massive spending on wellness and incentives that somehow escape inclusion in your actual healthcare budget—your prevention, control, and early detection spending is rising. But increases in these preventive categories are not being offset by reductions in surgeries, inpatient days, and emergency room visits, that (unless you've raised your ER visit copay to $100 or more, which has nothing to do with these so-called solutions you are being sold) have stayed the same for years except, if you are a small company, for some random bouncing. Ergo, you've accomplished nothing.

It's not just the spending. As the opening paragraph indicates, it's about employee* health, too. Sure, people can die from not getting adequate medical attention, but for the commercially insured

---

* Some companies refer to their employees as "associates," "people," "staff," and so on, instead of "employee," but for clarity I will be using the word employee through this book. The word is also shorthand for all covered people, included dependents.

population the following is only a slight exaggeration: Too much healthcare can kill you.

Many books, including those listed in the Bibliography, vividly illustrate that point. It's not just too much treatment. It's not just too much diagnosis. It's also too much prevention. That may sound like another Yogi Berra quote—how can you have too much prevention? Well, too much of anything is bad for you. Prevention—in the form of wellness programs and especially health fairs and biometric screens— turns out to be a substantial and largely unappreciated waste of money. More importantly, if you go too far, it's not just wasting your money: at some point you are less likely to help your employees than harm them, as the state of Nebraska example in Chapter 5 illustrates.

Cracking Health Costs describes what you can do to mitigate this epidemic of prevention, diagnosis, and treatment, by spending less profligately but more wisely. When I say "you" in this book and point out ways to spend your money more productively, I am assuming you are the CEO, COO, or CFO and have some control over how your money is spent. (Or, you are a very enlightened and analytically savvy benefits administrator or human resources executive who views the job as a steppingstone to senior management rather than something to do between rounds of golf with your benefits consultant.)

Unfortunately, there are scores of people feeding at your trough, people who benefit only if you do the opposite: spend more profligately but less wisely. Do not expect them to stand idly by while you cut back. I'm* talking not just about your vendors, carriers, and consultants. I'm also talking about the many people whom you never even come into direct contact with, such as pharmaceutical reps calling on doctors, radiologists getting paid by the scan, malpractice lawyers who want all bases covered, drug companies paying researchers to write positive journal articles, and advertising agencies convincing your employees to demand more pills. (As Governor Rick Scott, the former CEO of Columbia/HCA observed: "How many businesses do you know that want to cut their revenue in half? That's why the healthcare system won't change the healthcare system.")

---

* To prevent confusion, "I" in this book means Tom Emerick. Al Lewis will be referred to by name in the third person.

These folks, directly or indirectly, can be very persuasive. You may think you've held back their tides, but you probably haven't. The simple test below is an easy way to find out. You can answer "yes," "no," or "I don't know" to the following questions. If you answer yes to at least 10 of these 15 questions, you don't need *Cracking Health Costs*.

First, some outcomes questions. Over the past five years, per 1,000 covered people across your *entire covered population*, not just motivated participants in specific programs:

1. Have your inpatient days fallen?
2. Has the number of imaging tests fallen?
3. Has the number of specialist visits declined?
4. Have your wellness-sensitive medical events declined?
5. Has your number of inpatient surgical procedures declined?
6. Has your number of vendored programs decreased, and are these programs so inherently appealing that you no longer need to bribe people with incentives to participate in them?
7. What is the "spread" per prescription between what your pharmacy benefit manager receives from you and what it spends on drug procurement?
8. Have you actually measured most of these items above?

   Next, some process questions:
9. Have your RFPs and reconciliations become clearer, shorter, less expensive—and according to the outcomes measurement gold standard *Why Nobody Believes the Numbers*—valid?
10. Are your consultants and vendors showing you much lower, more realistic, ROIs for programs than they previously did, and focusing on the validity of those ROIs according to that gold standard?
11. Do you sleep well the night before you need to present your ROIs/outcomes to your boss, knowing that you'll be able to answer any tough question about your calculation?
12. Did your consultant inform you that there is no evidence that spending money on wellness will reduce healthcare spending, and/or did your vendor or consultant tell you that any differential spending reduction by participants, as compared to nonparticipants, is solely the result of self-selection by motivated people wanting to participate?

13. Do the hospitals in your network have higher Leapfrog safety scores than other hospitals in your marketplace, or did they get into your network solely on the basis of price or reputation?

14. Does your benefits design favor hospitals in your network that pay specialists salaries in order to discourage them from performing unnecessary procedures that would otherwise generate revenue?

15. Did your consultant or broker give you or recommend to you this book or the prequel? (Obviously your wellness vendor didn't.)

Okay, now tally your score.

The bad news is that you may have missed many of them, but the good news is, you're not alone. Probably a third of you answered "no" or "I don't know" to 10 or more. Well, that's why this book was written.

Cracking Health Costs will show you how to improve both your score, and more importantly, the cost-effectiveness of your health benefit. Most of what I'll be suggesting are easy things to eliminate. We'll explain why eliminating them will not only save you money but improve the health of your employees. In addition, these are primarily items your employees literally put zero value on. In the case of health advocacy, your employees actively want you uninvolved and often privately pay on their own even though you offer the benefit. If you wanted to find a new psychiatrist because you felt like your depression was getting worse, would you want your boss's health advocate company to help?

The good news is that subtracting a ton of worthless, counter-productive, and even harmful spending—offset by a small dollop of valuable spending—might be enough to reveal that rather than being an expensive annoyance, your health benefit is a valuable cost-containment and employee health tool. And just in time, too, because, like those immortal philosophers The Clash, your organization will soon need to answer the question: "Should I stay or should I go?" I can't remember what The Clash was referring to originally, but soon you'll be facing this choice with respect to the insurance exchanges. The exchanges provide an opportunity to trade the annual headache of benefits design for the annual headache of simply deciding how much to subsidize healthcare for your employees, and then sending your employees out on their own to the exchange, check in hand. Or you could pay the statutory penalty and not offer insurance at all. Or you could move people to part-time status and let them go on Medicaid. Even The Clash wasn't faced with this many choices.

Many vendors and consultants will lose a great deal of income if you decide to punt and use the exchange (though licensed broker-of-record fees are protected and not rebatable, so the cost of using one will fall on the carrier, until they raise their rates to cover it). Consequently, expect a full-court press from salespeople telling you how much money you can save, how employee morale is enhanced, how you can improve employee productivity by continuing to self-insure and adding some more prevention programs and so on. No doubt they'll pepper these proposals with the usual clichés, like how the "key takeaway" is that you'll create a "win-win" for "all the stakeholders."

On the other hand, your CFO will do the math, as CFOs are wont to do (no wonder they never get invited to parties) and may come to the conclusion that it is cheaper to pay the penalty . . . except that the penalty option is an either-or covering *all* full-time employees, including the aforementioned CFO. You can't create two classes of healthcare within your organization, a gold-plated one for the suits and foisting the full-time people who actually do the work onto Medicaid. Therefore, unless the Howells want to be cast adrift with Gilligan, you better make sure that you've exhausted all the possibilities for making your own benefit as cost-effective as possible before pursuing that option. And exploring the possibilities is exactly what this book is for. (You can avoid some of this by going to a higher mix of part-timers, but there are obvious limits to that.)

Taken as a whole, my view is, other things equal, there could be many reasons you would prefer to self-insure your employees and administer a health benefit rather than simply subsidize their use of an exchange or pay the penalty. After all, you switched to self-insurance to gain added control over the benefit. Why throw that away? At least *try* some of what *Cracking Health Costs* recommends to see if you can impact your health spending. The insurance exchanges will still be here next year, so you can always switch later. Switching now and then changing your mind and switching back is tougher. You lose your institutional knowledge of running a health benefit, just like companies that outsourced their manufacturing have lost their institutional knowl-edge of how to put things together. So innovation should be done earlier rather than later. (There are some exceptions to this self-insured recommendation that Chapter 11, which talks about exchanges, covers.)

I'm not advocating innovation for innovation's sake, though. *Cracking Health Costs* concludes that probably 90 percent of what you are getting sold is counterproductive at worst and worthless at best. Or, if not worthless, then not a large enough savings driver to merit the investment of time and money.

And that line provides an excellent segue into the chapter sum-mary, because you'll find that more chapters are much more about what's been oversold and doesn't work than about good ideas to implement, though we have plenty of those, too. *Cracking Health Costs* is divided into two parts, plus a conclusion. Part I, "Mostly Bad News," mostly pulls the curtain away from the army of vendors, consultants, and providers lined up to separate you and your employees from their money, offering little in return. Part II, "Mostly Good News," is much shorter, unfortunately. But there are some best practices out there worth investigating.

Chapter 1 provides a brief overview of the 90 percent of vendor interventions that are worthless, and explains why they are. (A few of the worthless items, because they are so popular, will also merit their own chapters later.) To some degree, Chapter 1 —as well as Chapter 3 on wellness—is a synopsis of my colleague and collaborator Al Lewis' award-winning trade bestseller *Why Nobody Believes the Numbers: Distinguishing Fact from Fiction in Population Health Management. Why Nobody Believes* is also funnier than *Cracking Health Costs,* which is intended as a serious volume for benefits administration and has an implementation emphasis. Plus, people undergoing unnecessary major surgeries are not funny, whereas claiming massive savings by bribing employees to eat more spinach is, especially when Al presents it.

Finally, look at the reviews for *Why Nobody Believes*—Al is simply much funnier than any other healthcare writer, period. Even though *Cracking Health Costs* is a serious book, a little of his style occasionally sneaks in. You think I came up with that Clash reference on my own? I wouldn't have thought to start a healthcare book with a reference to

The Clash, partly because that's not my style and partly because I've never heard of them. (Al came up with that last line, too.)

No doubt you've been sold a lot of vendor interventions because your brokers are making fat commissions off them, and that's the subject of Chapter 2. There's a reason why so many things look good to your brokers. It's because they are good—for your broker. Yes, there are some honest brokers and consultants. We've found a handful and you can use this chapter (as well as that 15-question diagnostic quiz you just took, which a good adviser will score close to 100 percent on) to see if yours fits the bill.

Ask yourself this single health benefit trivia question to see if indeed your consultants actually know enough about health benefits to be consulting you on the topic: Does your consultant being paid to advise you on how to reduce your heart attack rate through cardiac disease management and wellness programs know what your heart attack rate is and whether it has declined faster or slower than average since your program(s) started? I didn't think so. By the end of Chapter 2, you should have developed some healthy skepticism about what you hear from your advisors, as some honest ones offer an inside view of many of their colleagues' business practices.

What Chapter 2 does for brokers and consultants, Chapter 3 does for wellness vendors. It describes what some companies have finally been noticing, which is that wellness almost invariably increases your costs (when all costs are included) and in some cases harms your employees.

Then, Chapter 4 will peel away some of the patina, to the extent that there is any left, from the pharmacy benefits management industry. The chapter shows you that the complexity of their contracts is designed to obfuscate, and judging from the stock performance of that industry, does so quite effectively. It also provides some novel ideas to reduce your drug spend generally and PBM spending in particular.

But wait . . . there's more. Now how much would you pay? Quite a bit, as in Chapter 5 we venture inside the walls of the doctors' offices and hospitals and learn why your employees' health is too important to be entrusted to providers. You'll see how your employees get sucked into the treatment trap, which can start with a screen or health fair yielding a false positive on a lab test, and end with an unnecessary surgery. In this country, specialist training, culture, and financial incentives favor action over thought, procedures over watchfulness, and technology over judgment. You're frequently an involuntary co-conspirator, too, as local provider organizations salivate over your health fairs and biometric screens, knowing that they will generate a steady stream of customers following up on possible (but, as it turns out, mostly inconsequential) health problems. And you needn't take my word for this. Call a few local hospitals and see how willing they are to sponsor these activities for you.

Fees and procedures feed the beast today, but, we are told, help is on its way in the form of new delivery systems: Patient-Centered Medical Homes and Accountable Care Organizations. Chapter 6 covers them together because they are both delivery models involving different provider organizational methods, electronic medical records, and initials. PCMHs are a waste of money. It's too early to tell with ACOs. If they work, the net savings will be minor, so you can afford to wait.

While you're waiting, we do have some solutions for you, and this brings us to Part II, "Mostly Good News."

There is a best-practice for inpatient care, and it doesn't involve legislated changes to the delivery system. Chapter 7 describes a Company-Sponsored Centers of Excellence (CSCOE) model, used by a fast-growing number of employers to prevent unnecessary surgeries not by denying, restricting, or complicating access to care, but by enhancing it. It turns out to be worth a lot of money to fly a few of your employees, on your nickel, to one of the handful of the country's hospitals that takes this approach.

Chapter 8 shows how even right in your own very neighborhood, you can find and nudge your employees to safer hospitals than the ones you are using now, according to the highest objective standard, the Leapfrog Group Hospital Safety Score. And in hospitals, safer means better. This chapter reveals the epidemic of medical errors in this country, but shows how you can select hospitals for your local network that actively work at—and succeed in—minimizing them. There are many ways of measuring hospital quality and this chapter strongly advocates for the one—avoiding medical errors—that saves you money and shields your employees from injury.

Even though hospital safety scores and shopping for centers of excellence are important, a lot of you still don't want to give up on keeping people out of hospitals generally, so it is fortunate that a coordinated care model, which concentrates all member-facing services in a single entity, does actually save money. You can expect roughly a 2 to 4 percent reduction in overall trend, mostly from reduced hospitalizations, within a year or so after its implementation. However, the coordinated care model is not like cranberry juice where specific proportions of specific ingredients must be included to earn the label "pure juice" (hence, Ocean Spray labels its offering a "Cranberry Juice Cocktail"). Nope. It's *caveat emptor* in the coordinated care world—anyone can claim to offer it, and many carriers and vendors do. Chapter 9 describes what constitutes the model and provides the checklist for determining if your carrier (or disease management/wellness vendor) is one of them.

We will step out of character and close Part II with a more positive evolution of/substitution for wellness. Chapter 10 takes the wellness question to the so-what-do-I-do-instead level. It describes how you may be able to improve your company's bottom line with a global well-being emphasis, an approach that you can be assured will work because your consultants and vendors will discourage you from undertaking it, since its focus on internal cultural changes yanks away the corporate trough that they've been feeding at. Well-being does have a catch. The catch is, you can't just pay people incentives, send out health risk assessments, offer coaching, provide nicotine patches, and give people pedometers. You need to actually *do* something. The well-being model encompasses financial and emotional as well as physical health as catalysts for productivity improvement, and also requires attention to the work environment. And you won't get an immediate health claims payoff—but you should see an improvement in performance, which matters more to your organization. The health claims payoff will come later.

I end with the conclusion and the question on whether to move to the exchanges. You might ask, "Time for the conclusion already? What about mental health, health savings accounts, high-deductible plans, narrow networks, and [fill in your own blank here]?"

Answer: I don't know anything about those topics so I wouldn't be doing you any favors by discussing them. Healthcare is an almost $3 trillion industry. No one can know it all. The good news is that understanding the topics in this book will spur you to ask the right questions when you evaluate those other topics. The critical thinking tools used in *Cracking Health Costs* can be applied broadly across the other healthcare services you use. And when you do evaluate these other services, you may reach the same conclusion I do regarding the topics covered in this book. That conclusion is [WARNING: SPOILER ALERT]: Keep vendors away from your checkbook, keep consultants away from your conference room, and keep providers away from your workforce.

And then just simply do the things suggested in this book. All told, you have an opportunity for an 8 to 10 percent reduction in claims costs. And to the extent your employees even notice these initiatives, they will thank you for them.

Part I

Mostly Bad News

Chapter 1

Myths and Facts about Your Health Benefit

One reason that your spending tends to rise so quickly is likely because a lot of what you think you know about controlling health expenses is mistaken. This shouldn't come as much of a surprise, given that few how-to articles and books are actually written by people who manage health benefits for a living. It is easy to say something saves money if you're the vendor selling it or the consultant getting paid to procure, implement, and evaluate it. But *actually* saving money is quite a bit more challenging. Most money-saving ideas pitched to you have one thing in common: they may or may not save money, but they do cost money. And the funny thing is that while the expense is always in hard dollars, the savings generally require some kind of reconciliation or outcomes report that's laden with assumptions and fallacies.

As one corporate medical director observed, "If all my programs got the return on investment that vendors say they achieved, I'd have negative medical spending."

Well, here's a news flash: you don't have negative medical spending, and this chapter will explain why. More important, it will explain the facts that will allow you to spend less than you are now while ensuring that your employees are better off.

The first two sets of myths and facts correspond with subsequent chapters that are referenced in each set. If you're reading this electronically, you can click through directly to the referenced chapter for a more in-depth discussion. If you're reading the hard copy, you'll have to leaf through the actual pages themselves to reach the chapter in question. (Wellness vendors would not consider this as a chore. They would call it finger aerobics and give you incentive payments for completing the task. Okay, not really, but the stuff they really do, as you'll see, isn't so different.) Not every chapter corresponds with a myth, though, because not every solution begins with a misunderstanding.

Likewise, not every myth corresponds with a chapter. The last set of myths is designed to stand alone, because the story ends there quite cleanly.

Finally, each myth/fact ends with a takeaway that you can act upon posthaste.

I: Myths Covered in Chapter 3: Yes, Even Wellness Can Be Hazardous to Your Health

Despite its many other contributions toward creating a culture of health (if done correctly), the concept of "increasing wellness" is pure mythology vis-à-vis your actual health spending. Hopefully, the five myth-busters here and a chapter on the topic later in the book will convince you of that.

Myth: Actively managing your health benefit and your employees' health will reduce disease and premature mortality.

Fact: Your actual management of your health benefit has surprisingly little influence on a given employee's health. Not none, just nowhere near as much as the amount of effort you put into it would suggest. The greatest determinants of health and longevity include genetics, socioeconomic status/finances, job satisfaction, behavioral risks, personal relationships, zip code, and luck. So the best way for an employer to improve health status and productivity is to create a workplace culture that employees want to be part of. You'll therefore find that we debunk many push-button programs that require vendors, whereas we recommend making internal cultural improvements. (However, Chapter 10 does suggest a comprehensive well-being solution that is partially vendored and goes far beyond wellness to address finances, job satisfaction, and other mitigable, non-health-related factors that contribute to overall well-being.)

Action implication: Spending more and doing more doesn't necessarily pay off. Gold-plated health plans often encourage overuse, overdiagnosis, and overtreatment. So don't be afraid to cut back. Many chapters provide suggestions for specific places to cut back on services you pay for now—and we promise that most employees won't even notice their absence.

Myth: Keeping people out of the hospital via a wellness program is the best way to reduce your health spending.

Fact: As described in Chapter 3 and at length in the companion volume, *Why Nobody Believes the Numbers*, there is not one shred of evidence that a corporate wellness program can reduce the cost of your health benefit at all, let alone by more than the cost of the program. If it can't do that, it certainly can't cover the cost of the average incentive payment, which itself usually exceeds all spending on all health risk-sensitive inpatient events that even the most perfect wellness program could possibly prevent. And chances are, your wellness program is anything but perfect. You are likely throwing large incentives and expensive programs at people who simply either aren't going to change in any meaningful way or would change (or maintain their good health) even without incentives. And there's just no way that any claims cost and productivity savings for the sliver of people in between who *do* change in response to incentives and the program itself would be able to offset the program spending on and incentives paid to everybody else.

Just as with health status as described above, most research suggests that the best way to reduce medical spending and absenteeism is to establish a culture that makes people *want* to go to work. Easier said than done, for sure; but reallocating the money that you would have spent on incentives (an average of $521 per person in the Fortune 500, according to the National Business Group on Health) toward internal cultural improvements or total well-being (as described in Chapter 10) is a start. The wellness chapter will propose that one step toward that goal is to redirect your spending from complex, outsourced, vendored programs involving health risk-oriented assessments and blood draws to internal cultural improvements that say "my company cares about me," even if they don't actually save money. One terrific example of this is Comcast's employee cafeteria. It offers employees a 360-degree view of Philadelphia, along with ambience and food that match those of many fine restaurants. It certainly saves money by enhancing productivity, in the sense that employees have no reason to want to go off-site to eat, and it certainly brightens their day—figuratively and, with floor-to-ceiling two-story windows 50-something floors up, literally. However, these aren't savings you're able to measure directly.

But don't just take my word for this. The next time you're addressing a group, ask people to raise their hands if they've had a health problem that could have been avoided by talking to a wellness coach. Next, ask people to raise their hands if they've ever been the victim of a medical error. You'll get 10 times the number of hands for the latter, and you'll see why *Cracking Health Costs* wants to focus you both on avoiding the errors themselves (through hospital selection) as well as the opportunity for those errors to occur in the first place (through discouraging overutilization of hospitals). Since little of what presents people with the opportunity to fall into the treatment trap can be prevented through wellness (and is sometimes itself the result of a wellness-generated health screen, as we'll see), *Cracking Health Costs* follows the money.

Action implication: Save money by curtailing your vendored wellness program, and see if it makes more economic sense to procure a scaled-down version directly from your health plan. Employees should still have access to the program, but don't pay or give them other incentives to coax them into doing something of no inherent interest or value to them. In the immortal words of the great philosopher Yogi Berra: "If people don't want to go to the ballpark, you can't stop them."

Myth: We shouldn't eliminate those incentives. We should raise them and tie them more closely to behavior change like the Affordable Care Act wants us to do.

Fact: Perhaps this might work on your planet. However, here on Earth, while you and your wellness vendors are handing out shareholders' money to people who promise to eat more broccoli, the tobacco and food industries are spending billions to figure out new ways of hooking your employees on their products without them even being aware this is happening.

If you still think incentives are any match for those industries' technological and financial resources, I might suggest reading "The Extraordinary Science of Addictive Junk Food," in the *New York Times* magazine (February 26, 2013). You'll learn that, against your incentives, the junk food industry is pouring billions of dollars into addiction science, studying and exploiting the brain's cravings for sweets and fats that have been evolving since the earliest primates roamed the earth. The wellness industry's counterattack: even *higher* incentives, on the theory that surely there is some amount employers can pay employees to cure an addiction they don't even know they have.

Action implication: Give up on incentives. Or find one reputable behavioral economist who thinks they work.

Myth: Even if a full-blown wellness coaching program is a waste of time and money, we should still get employees to complete health risk assessments (HRAs).

Fact: Who decreed that HRAs were going to solve the United States' healthcare crisis? For most people, these things are a complete waste of their time and—especially if you pay people to complete them, like many companies do—your money. (The people who wouldn't be wasting their time and might learn something are also the people who don't complete them in the first place.)

Here's how an HRA works: if you smoke, the feedback printout from your HRA will tell you to stop smoking. If you don't wear a seat belt, you'll receive a printout telling you to wear a seat belt. (And, in an ideal world, since almost every car beeps and buzzes until you do, you would also get a printout telling you to test your hearing.) If your employees are so un-self-aware that they don't realize they should stop smoking or wear seat belts until an HRA tells them to—well, then, you probably should have hired different employees.

One other point: people lie on these things. Yes, you know you don't read their responses, but *they* don't know that. (They do know you can read their private e-mails.) You can reassure them of this a thousand times, but odds are that they'll still lie, just in case you are. Think about it—wouldn't you? Especially when the question is: "How many times did you drive drunk last year?"

Action implication: You can take the same approach as you do with the wellness program. Free HRAs can be found online at sites like at www.realage.com. Let people know where to find them, and offer assistance in interpreting results—and leave it at that.

Myth: Fewer healthcare dollars are spent on slender people and nonsmokers over their lifetimes than on overweight smokers. Therefore, our company should incentivize people to enroll in weight loss and smoking cessation programs.

Fact: The facts are much more nuanced than they're made to seem in this oft-cited and oversimplified claim. While healthier people will, on average, spend less on medical care than unhealthy people, this is not true by as much of a margin as one might expect, until people hit the magic Medicare-eligible age, at which point they're not your problem. It also doesn't logically follow from the fact that healthy people cost less than unhealthy people that you can somehow pay unhealthy people to become healthy. By way of analogy, Germans are more productive than Greeks, but no one has suggested that Greece's economic crisis can be solved if the European Union pays Greeks to take classes to learn how to behave like Germans. Paying unhealthy people to take classes to learn to act like healthy people is only a slightly less ill-considered idea. Nonetheless, enough benefits managers think that, figuratively speaking, they can turn Greeks into Germans that the wellness industry sells about $6 billion/year of completely ineffectual interventions to corporate human resources departments that fail to appreciate this fallacy.

Action implication: Instead of succumbing to a get-well-quick scheme proffered by a vendor, consider a more measured, less expensive, internally focused approach. Some portion of your workforce does patrol its own health. Another portion is perfectly content being unhealthy and won't change on its own, absent a wake-up call like a sibling dropping dead of a heart attack. In between are people who would like to improve their health but just haven't prioritized it, either due to time or economics. For much less money than it costs to pay everyone to complete a health risk assessment, you could subsidize healthier food choices in the cafeteria. You can take dietary economics a step further by using one of the companies that will subsidize healthy food choices in local supermarkets. Food is like anything else: people respond to economics. If you make healthier food cheaper, people will buy more of it. (It is not clear that they will also buy less unhealthy food, though. Subsidies always encourage overuse.)

Time is often an issue when it comes to fitness. Therefore, bringing fitness to the workers via on-site facilities will encourage more participation than simply paying for gym memberships. One caution borne of experience: company locker rooms need to emphasize privacy. Many people who have no problem getting naked in an anonymous gym locker room will nonetheless balk at the idea of their colleagues seeing them in the buff.

And, as mentioned earlier, if you really want people to improve their productivity and health, focus on the more basic human resources function of reducing stress and increasing happiness in the workplace—hence our exposition of "well-being" as a grown-up version of wellness in Chapter 10. Any other get-well-quick vendor schemes are merely distractions from this much more effective approach.

II: Myths Covered at Length in Other Chapters

Myth: Okay, maybe self-reported data is a waste of time, but blood values don't lie. We should do biometric screenings and encourage diagnostic tests.

Fact: For every story you hear of someone whose risk factors were very high and didn't know it, there are a hundred stories you don't hear of people rushing off to the doctor due to a false positive on some kind of screen or diagnostic. False positives are shockingly common. A lab test with 95 percent accuracy sounds like almost a lock. But suppose you are testing for an asymptomatic abnormality present in 1 in every 10,000 people. Yes, you'll likely find that 1 if you test those 10,000 people; but you'll also get 500 false positives, because 95 percent accurate also means 5 percent inaccurate. In other words, even people who test positive would have only a 1 in 500 chance of actually having this abnormality. Those other 499 will go to the doctor and get followed up on, wasting their time and your money—not to mention adding unnecessary angst to their lives.

There are other drawbacks, too. If you make screening voluntary, the people who won't go to the doctor won't be tested, either. Make it mandatory, and you risk an employee-relations issue. Paying people to be screened helps—except for what turns out to be the very considerable expense, and even then you'll miss exactly the people you want to capture.

Action implication: No more paying people to be screened. Spending the incentive on workplace enhancements instead has the other advantage of not generating taxable income. But after you finish this book, you may not want to be screening at all. . . .

Myth: Don't put off doctor visits and wait for a problem to get worse.

Fact: I've found, while running large company benefit operations, that a huge percentage of impromptu doctor visits are for things that would go away on their own. And primary care doctors to whom I've spoken confirm this claim. If people would apply common sense to doctor visits, we could eliminate a great deal of waste. How many millions of visits involve the common cold, which, as the joke goes, could take a whole week to go away if you don't go to the doctor but only seven days if you do? And some doctors will still prescribe antibiotics for colds, driving costs up further while introducing unnecessary and potentially harmful drugs into your employees' bodies.

All family doctors have patients who see them for frivolous reasons—individuals who are colloquially known as "frequent flyers." Given the number of visits they make, some of them will inevitably receive a prescription for an expensive medication—and have costly and sometimes risky tests. Why are there so many frequent flyers in healthcare? It's simple: because others—defined as you and me—foot the bill for their visits.

My own experience and observations aren't the only claims evidence that going to the doctor is overrated. According to *American Medical News* (October 15, 2012), the rate of physician visits for adults under 65 fell 19 percent between 2001 and 2010. During that same decade, the rate of emergency room visits and hospitalizations for the five, common, chronic conditions (asthma, coronary artery disease, congestive heart failure, chronic obstructive pulmonary disease, and diabetes) fell by a similar percentage. While one couldn't infer causality from that correlation, one could certainly infer the opposite: staying away from the doctor doesn't increase one's likelihood of getting sick enough to require emergency or inpatient care.

One "natural experiment"—an experiment for which Al is the country's leading evaluation expert (which is why he is making me cite it three times in this book, so don't roll your eyes at *me* when it comes up twice again*)—did, in fact, determine that increased access to physicians increases cost without reducing emergency and inpatient care. At considerable taxpayer expense, North Carolina has steadily and dramatically increased physician access for its Medicaid enrollees since the late 1990s, while South Carolina hasn't. And yet, for overall hospitalizations, as well as for the set of conditions that the government says are most responsive to outpatient care, South Carolina Medicaid's admission rate has performed better than North Carolina's since 2001. Note that Medicaid recipients are historically considered to be the most in need of access, which indicates that if any population could benefit

---

* Also, just before we went to press, the state, acknowledging that Al was right and their high-priced name-brand consultants were wrong, announced their intention to scale back or even dismantle the program. Unfortunately, we need to score one for Al. I say "unfortunately" because he was already insufferable enough on this topic before this happened.

from increased access, they certainly could. Even so, it appeared more likely than not (though not statistically significant) that physician visits were at least to a slight degree driving hospital admission rates higher rather than preventing them.

Action implication: Don't incentivize people to go to the doctor; they'll do it plenty on their own. This includes so-called preventive visits, which as renowned Reuters health/science writer Sharon Begley observed (January 29, 2013), don't prevent much at all.

Myth: If something is seriously wrong with an employee, especially a C-suite employee, that person should have access to the best hospitals in the country, as measured by *U.S. News & World Report* or *Consumer Reports* surveys.

There are three kinds of goods and services. You can judge the quality of one kind before the fact, like a couch. That is, you buy a couch after you sit on it in the showroom and decide it's comfortable. The second kind is experiential: you decide whether a restaurant is good after you eat there once or twice. Healthcare uniquely occupies a third category: a service whose quality you often can't measure even after you've experienced it.

Consequently, these reputational surveys of users (or, in the case of *U.S. News*, mostly nonusers) correlate only loosely with a hospital's actual quality. Why should a large hospital in a big city automatically be considered high-quality merely because people have heard of it? This is why we devote a chapter to hospital quality and why it should matter to you. We highlight some of the best hospitals you've never heard of and show you how to cost-effectively add them to your network.

III: Myths that End Here

Myth: Disease management will help you save money by keeping sick people out of the hospital.

Fact: If wellness is defined as attempting to make your whole company healthier, disease management (DM) is focused on individuals with identified health issues. As with wellness, there are a few success stories of people who really don't know how to manage their condition and, hence, benefit from disease management. The differences—and why DM has intrinsic merit, even if insurance carriers and vendors oversell it—are that DM programs (1) focus on people who already have major health issues and (2) don't throw money at people in an attempt to bribe them into getting better. As a result, DM should more than pay for itself.

But intrinsic merit is not enough for your carrier and/or vendor, which will almost inevitably show you massive savings from DM using their "reconciliation methodology," which they (with approval from your consultants) have designed to overstate savings. The reason for this overstatement can be best described via analogy. Suppose everyone who had a past medical event is a "heads" while people who, unknown to you or them, are at risk for their first medical event are "tails." Last year, the heads were much higher cost than the tails, specifically because they had a medical event. Vendors and consultants only measured the heads—the people they knew about—and half of them would flip to low-cost tails on their own. So lots of heads are shown going from high-cost to low-cost, which overstates the savings by ignoring the people flipping the other way. In all cases, the reconciliation methodology measures only the previously high-cost people. Sometimes "high-risk," "complex," or "identified" replaces "previously high-cost," but those are all just synonyms for "a group whose costs will come down on their own even if you do nothing, the same way some heads will flip to tails."

Only the downward regression to the mean is baked in, because it's almost impossible to predict the opposite: which people who were too low-cost to be found in your database will nonetheless have a major medical event. If you had a magic transponder to pinpoint the people you can't find because they don't have claims but who were going to have an event nonetheless, you could offset the savings from the high-cost people declining with the added expenses of previously low-cost people having events. But you don't have a magic transponder—so the savings are made up. The arithmetic behind this observation is outside the scope of this book, but is covered in *Why Nobody Believes the Numbers*.

Action implication: Vendors and consultants generally want you to pay a per-employee-per-month fee for these services, and/or pay for everyone who doesn't actively opt out. However, it is much cheaper and equally effective to simply pay for the people who most want to use the service, instead of forcing people to tell you that they don't want it. The folks who opt in should benefit—cost-effectively from your point of view—from the added information and support.

Myth: The 10 percent of people with chronic disease account for 80 percent of your health spending. Managing them is the first step toward controlling your overall costs.

Fact: There are certain facts you need to commit to memory, the kind of facts you need to have at your fingertips, because in this hypercharged, dog-eat-dog survival-of-the-fittest economy, they give you a major advantage over competitors and coworkers who don't know them. However, this "10/80 rule" is not one of those facts. It's more like the opposite, the kind of cliché people spout when they want to sound smart but don't actually know anything. Here's the upshot. First, that 80 percent canard covers *all* costs incurred by people with chronic disease, such as someone with asthma having a baby. Second, that 80 percent also covers people whose chronic diseases are not the usual cardiometabolic ones but are rare diseases that they control using specially developed "orphan drugs" at great expense. There's little you can do to reduce that expense further, because it's already driven by preventive medication.

Third, speaking of prevention, a huge chunk of this 80 percent generally is already being spent on drugs and other preventive measures. For instance, you are spending literally 10 times as much on drugs for asthma as you are spending on emergency room and inpatient claims for asthma. And yet consultants keep telling you to spend even more, in order to reduce emergency room visits still further. What they won't tell you—because they've never done the straightforward math—is that you'll spend about 10 times as much to prevent additional ER and inpatient use by asthmatics not already taking their drugs than the occasional "crash" would cost. You have to medicate a lot of unmedicated mild asthmatics in order to prevent a single one from crashing. Because doctors (and certainly disease managers) can't predict who is going to have an attack, they often medicate people only *after* they've had an attack on the statistically surprisingly unlikely theory that they are going to have another one, rather than beforehand when it would have done some good. In that sense, trying to predict and prevent asthmatics from going to the ER is a bit like whack-a-mole. And as with most other overtreatment and overprevention issues, it's not just the expense. It's all those drugs being introduced into people's bodies, day after day.

I'm not saying you should discourage asthmatics from taking their drugs. I'm simply suggesting that you should avoid incentives that interfere with, or attempt to outthink, the natural doctor-patient relationship when it comes to drugs for diseases like these. Doctors will overprescribe plenty on their own, without prodding from you.

Fourth, that 80 percent was spent on *last year's* 10 percent—people who won't overlap much with this year's 10 percent. Once again, a whack-a-mole situation—you'll be focused on last year's high utilizers. Worse, if you find a vendor to manage last year's 10 percent, it will claim credit for the reduction in its costs, which, of course, would have fallen anyway as others take their place in this year's 10 percent generating the 80 percent.

This classic vendor trick of saying "send us your sickest patients and watch us reduce their costs" has been around in one form or another for almost 20 years. Yet it still seems to work, as benefits departments have almost no institutional memory.

There is, however, one situation where addressing the 10/80 rule works, and that's where you identify some of those 10 percent *before* they incur their costs. Not through predictive modeling, which is bogus enough to earn its own entry as the next myth, but rather through referrals to Company-Sponsored Centers of Excellence (CSCOEs), the use of which proactively prevents some of those costs. CSCOEs are an important enough part of the solution to merit their own chapter.

Action implication: Commit this section to memory, as the 10/80 rule comes up time and time again in one form or another and is always wrong. Show the door to any vendor that promises to reduce costs for people who are high-risk, high-cost, complex, or any adjective derived from last year's spending.

Myth: Predictive modeling can identify the people who will benefit from our interventions.

Fact: If there were a reality show to pick healthcare's biggest fraud, the runner-up to wellness would be predictive modeling based on claims data. The only question about debunking predictive modeling is where to start. To begin, consider two people with identical amounts of plaque in their arteries and other risk factors. The first is on medication and has had a stress test and therefore—since you need a test, procedure, or event to get a heart disease diagnosis—has been identified as a heart patient. The other hasn't been to the doctor for a preventive physical in 20 years.

The second person is far more likely to crash. However, the predictive model will pick up only the first—ironically, largely because that person is patrolling his health closely enough to seek a diagnosis and treatment. It will recommend that you focus disease management on that person, which we know is the exact opposite of what should happen. This second person is not hypothetical: I just described television journalist Tim Russert, fitness revolution leader Jim Fixx, and any number of other people who simply dropped dead from sudden heart attacks but who never would have been predicted to do so by a claims-based model for the simple reason that they didn't have any claims. (Jim Fixx, for one, was in total denial of doctors' advice he had received before he starting running.)

Next, assume you do go to the doctor, who examines you, tests you, and tells you your risks. They are just that: risks. Even your doctor can't give you a "yes" or "no" on whether you are going to fall victim to a heart attack, let alone when. If your own doctor can't predict that you'll have a heart attack or other event, how can someone who has never even met you do so simply by looking at your medical claims? Oh, and did I mention that these medical claims are usually three months out of date? And that while these medical claims summaries do indicate whether someone has had a lab test, they don't disclose those tests' results? How useful is the former without the latter? It would be like a contestant on *Let's Make a Deal* knowing that there is something behind Door Number One but having no clue what it is—and then trying to use it as collateral.

Action implication: If someone wants to sell you a predictive model, give him last year's data and see how well he would have predicted this year's utilizers. Since anyone can straight-line last year's high utilizers to predict some of them to be this year's high utilizers, too, see how well the model predicts the low-to-high utilizers. *That* is true prediction.

Myth: On-site clinics will reduce your medical spending and increase your productivity because employees don't have to go off-site to the doctor.

Fact: The good news is that, unlike most of the other myths in this chapter, this one is not obviously a total fallacy. If you substituted on-site medical visits for trips to the doctor on a one-for-one basis, you'd certainly save money, because the latter cost much more than the former.

But in real life using this approach increases total physician visits, for various reasons: the visits are usually free, the doctor is right there, and many people would rather go to the doctor than do their jobs. Still, even if doctor visits climbed somewhat, you'd be ahead of the game if the cost savings/visit offsets the extra utilization. "Somewhat" is a vague word, specifically because the actual break-even number of extra visits depends on many factors: what you pay now per visit; how many of the new visits generate prescriptions and specialist referrals; whether you pay employees their hourly rate to miss work for doctor visits; whether they will make up the lost work on their own or you'll have to pay someone to do it; or how acutely the person's absence will be felt, like in an inbound call center, where short staffing can increase hold times.

Very few consultants and self-insured organizations actually run the numbers on these variables. Instead, they simply compare the cost per visit for off-site, to the cost per visit for on-site, as Wisconsin's Beloit School District did. As reported in the *Beloit Daily News* (September 4, 2012), the district saved about $419 on each of the 670 on-site clinic visits by its employees versus what it would have spent if they had gone to the doctor for those same visits. According to this logic, each additional visit to an on-site clinic saves about $419; therefore, more visits generate more savings. This logic is a little like Subtraction Stew in *The Phantom Tollbooth*, where the more you eat, the hungrier you get. (A savings of $419 per visit also suggests the district needs to renegotiate its existing physician contracts.)

While it is not clear—and it will vary by situation—whether on-site clinics save money, we do know three things for certain. First, on-site clinics won't help you manage your chronically ill employees much, if at all. You'll learn this if you try getting an on-site clinic vendor to go "at risk" for chronic disease events. The vendor will make all sorts of marketing representations but won't guarantee a reduction in those events in the contract. And for good reason: while many employees would stop by an on-site clinic for sprained ankles or an acute illness, few want your doctor involved in their ongoing health issues.

Second, it boggles the mind how many vendors will try to pitch on-site clinics in decidedly subscale workplaces that may only have 500 or 1,000 employees on-site. Consider a grouping of 1,000 employees. Figure half will prefer their own doctor even if the on-site doctor visits are free. Half of the remaining half will only use on-site clinics for urgent care needs during work hours, and/or won't want to discuss their ongoing personal issues with a doctor their employer is paying. Once you remove those potential visits from the mix, you don't have enough visits to cover the cost of the clinic. And this assumes that remaining quarter works the day shift when the clinic would be open.

Third, there is some good news. The exact issues that make on-site medical clinics questionable are what make on-site *dental* clinics a winner. While some people may prefer going to the doctor to going to work, no one prefers going to the dentist to anything not involving the IRS or their exes. This means that you won't generate extra visits, and dentists rarely prescribe or refer to specialists (and when they do, it is likely needed, if not overdue), so you won't generate extra ancillaries. You still have an economy-of-scale issue, though, which doesn't go away unless the dental clinic vendor can offer less than full-time care. Onsite Health (www.onsitehealth.com) is one vendor that does this; it allows employees to schedule dentist appointments a few days per week or month when either a mobile dental practice or a fully self-contained portable dental unit is on-site. With the rare exception, such as an abscess, dental issues are typically unlike medical issues in that even most urgent ones can wait a few days. A toothache isn't going to get better on its own; but your employee will almost never crash from it, either.

There is even a unique second high note in this myth-busting chapter: dental or medical, a clinic tells your employees you care about them. And remember the mantra from earlier in this section: make your investments in employee health visible and convenient, because you are trying to create a workplace that tells your employees they matter. Despite the other controversies surrounding them, clinics are visible and convenient.

Action implications: First, poll your employees to gauge interest and only enter into a contract if you are at scale, based on employee count and interest. Second, when measuring outcomes, don't use Beloit's Subtraction Stew approach. Count total doctor visits—on-site and off-site—as well as cost per visit, and compare to the baseline numbers for both. And don't overlook the hidden costs of physician visits at either site—prescriptions, tests, and referrals coming out of these visits. The true cost of a physician visit takes into account these downstream effects, as one clinical provider, We Care TLC (www .wecaretlc.com), does. Finally, check into dental as an alternative or complement to on-site medical.

We Care TLC: A Standout in the Field

Like most of the categories covered in *Cracking Health Costs*, there is no shortage of vendors for corporate medical clinics. Different vendors will fit different needs, but we are highlighting We Care TLC.* While this program—along with every other vendor in every other category—will itself offer multiple reasons it is unique, we like it because one of the principals, Brian Klepper, is also a reimbursement expert (quoted at length later in the book on that topic). Brian embedded mechanisms in his clinics' management controls and physician contracts to prevent patients from falling into the "treatment trap"—that is, receiving inappropriate and unnecessary referrals from their clinics to overpriced, perversely incentivized specialists and surgeons. And the We Care clinics themselves include all services (such as lab tests) on an all-in-one-price basis, which means that their incentives are aligned with yours as the buyer and, hence, quite consistent with the model we espouse for providers generally.

Myth: Access to a 24/7 nurse triage line will reduce emergency room visits.

[Pause.] Sorry about the delay there. I was laughing too hard to write. First, have you ever counted your ER visits before and after implementing this program? I'm guessing you haven't—so go do that now. [Pause again while you do this.] Notice any reduction? I didn't think so. (If there is a reduction, I'd be willing to bet that you raised copays along the way, too, which is the main reason ER visits are declining.) The nurse triage line vendor's job is to *pretend* that you reduced ER visits. Vendors do that by showing you a report that says "here's what people say they would have done if they hadn't called this

---

* Note that a "highlight" is not an endorsement. This book doesn't "endorse," where endorse is defined as, "We have reviewed all the vendors and these folks are the best." Rather, "highlight" is more like: "We know this vendor and believe it to be worthy of a serious investigation in most situations, but we can't guarantee that you won't find another vendor whose offering in the category in question fits your needs better."

line," with some large number of people claiming that they would have visited the emergency room.

Al once did a forensic review of a case in which the number of people saying they would have visited the ER was actually quite a bit larger than the actual number of emergency room visits the year before the program started. Additionally, the number of ER visits didn't decline at all after the program was implemented. So the vendor's claim was impossible two different ways: the number of ER visits they claimed to have avoided exceeded the number even available to be avoided, and the program had no impact, anyway.

Second, focus for a minute on what you paid for this service per-employee-per-month versus the number of times you (or your employees) use it. Look at the aforementioned vendor report. Did your vendor do the obvious math and divide the annual fee by the number of phone calls to calculate your cost per phone call? Once again, I didn't think so. If you do this math, you'll see that these 10-minute phone calls cost you about $100 apiece. In one case, so few phone calls were made that the employer would have spent less if there was no phone option and every caller simply went to the ER instead. In another case, a major health plan executive (finally) did the math for its $7 million a year program, and told its vendor: "I've just reviewed the data for the last three years and concluded that you've basically stolen $21 million from us."

Third, these people have liability issues, too, you know—and those liability issues often *increase* ER visits. Al had the following unpleasant experience upon calling a 24/7 nurse triage line one morning when he woke up with vertigo. All he wanted was answers to a couple of questions and a physician referral. Five minutes later he found himself in the back of an ambulance. Apparently there is a 1 percent chance that vertigo signals a stroke—and although he's a triathlete and Ultimate Frisbee player with zero risk factors for stroke, they had to rule out that possibility with a $2,000 ambulance ride to the $1,000 ER. These vendors often brag during their sales presentation about how they've never been sued—and this is why. No matter what the cost to you or the inconvenience to your employees, they don't take chances.

This is not an isolated story. I once installed a nurse triage line for a company and saw the ER visit rate go way up afterward. Problem was, it's easy and nearly risk free to the vendor to recommend an ER visit to callers. It was also profitable for the vendor, as the call times went way down, as well. Obviously the program was cancelled quickly, because we had the sense to run the numbers. You might suggest to your consultants that they dust off their calculators and try it sometime.

Action implication: Review your reports, do the arithmetic, and then take the following step: change the vendor contract to per-call pricing, at about $30 a phone call. You'll save about 70 percent with no negative impact on employees.

Myth: Maybe 24-hour lines are a waste of money and our employees don't use them, but our healthcare advocacy lines are a valuable service. Our employees use them.

Fact: Unlike calls to 24-hour lines, which at least end with an action step for the caller, those healthcare advocacy "incoming call" figures are hugely inflated by calls from people who didn't get what they wanted. For instance, my friend Bob called to find an oncologist for his mother, who lived across the country. The list he got was form-generated. He could have gotten those names online, and, in any event, none of them took Medicare.

Bob's wasn't a sensitive personal issue, but when employees really do have a personal health issue, do you seriously think they are going to call people who you don't just pay, but specifically pay to control your health spending? To tell these people their depression has gotten worse? To ask where to get an HIV test? Obviously you and I know that these healthcare advocates aren't making a list of these calls and emailing it to your board of directors, but your employees can't be sure. Someone calling one of these numbers has a lot on his mind and does not feel the need to add job insecurity to that list. Also, most of these numbers are available only during business hours, so people would need to call from their cubicles to discuss their prostate test results? I think not.

The way you can tell your services aren't being used is by looking at the massive growth in private, standalone B-to-C health advocacy services, which are usually local to an area and don't work through employers. They often send someone to the home, after hours, to have the conversation. (An example would be www.pathfindersmedical.com, if you'd like to get a closer look at true health advocacy. They were the ones who ended up finding Bob's mother a suitable oncologist by working through a network of other advocates.)

So if you want to be helpful, drop the per-employee-per-month subscription service that you're using now. You aren't just paying for a service that's not appreciated. You're paying for a service that your employees actively don't want you to provide. Surely there are better ways to spend that money. It would be hard to imagine a worse one.

Myth: As a cost reduction strategy, auditing is soooo premillennial. These days automated software and the carriers/ TPAs take care of finding overpayments/ineligible employees, and so on, so there's no reason to pay for it.

Fact: Auditing of eligibility, claims, workers compensation bills, stop loss, and vendor programs can reduce annual healthcare costs by 3 percent or more. For example, a recent audit of "hours worked" identified 3 percent of employees as ineligible for medical benefits since they failed to meet the "minimum hours worked" requirement. In another example, nearly $500,000 was erroneously paid because a TPA didn't realize that an employee on dialysis had become Medicare-eligible.

But don't take our word for this opportunity. There is at least one vendor—www.HRbestpractices.com—that not only takes contingency payments for audits but also leaves the savings calculation on which the contingency payment is based completely in your hands. You can stiff them for any reason—you can tell them it's because the Yankees (pick one) lost/won/were rained out—and there's not a darn thing, contractually speaking, they can do about it. The fact that vendors willing to do this even exist means that auditing should be a gold mine for you.

As Benefits Administrators, What Should We Do Next?

Read the remaining chapters. The action steps in this one are easy because they primarily involve doing less of things that don't work. They require no budget—and honestly, most employees won't even notice these changes (unless your incentive payment to complete HRAs was so high they count on it every year, in which case you'll need a communications plan to disengage gently). Part I, "Mostly Bad News," recommends clearing your plate of worthless interventions and creating a pool of resources so that you will be well-positioned to get the most out of Part II, "Mostly Good News."

Chapter 2

Does Your Broker or Consultant Have Your Back?

Just like everyone else, benefits consultants and brokers need to make money. And they rarely make money by advising clients to "do nothing"—even though that's often the right answer. They usually want you to do *something*, even if it makes no sense. For instance, one consulting firm was able to convince a large hospital system to put its disease management program out for bid—thereby generating a large fee for itself—even though the health plan that was already providing the service for that hospital system had received an award for having the lowest adverse medical event rates in common chronic disease categories in the country, arguably making it the United States' most effective health plan at disease management. But that's not the punch line; the punch line is that the *hospital system owned the health plan that its consultant advised it to procure a bid against.*

This is just one example of consultants gone wild, and others would be anything having to do with wellness. Benefits consultants, and especially brokers, don't make money if a company tries to create a culture of wellness, because they don't need a vendor in these cases. This is why and how fee-generating vendored get-well-quick schemes proliferate, while too few companies undergo the more challenging, but ultimately more rewarding, attempt to transition to a culture of wellness.

Few would deny the importance—and the difficulty—of creating a wellness-oriented culture. But given a choice between encouraging you, your supervisor (who oversees human resources), and the C-suite denizens who set the tone and allocate the resources to create this culture on the one hand and generating a brokerage fee to bring in a vendor on the other, few advisors (we will use "advisors" as a short-hand for benefits consultants and brokers) will opt for the route that doesn't generate a fee. This is especially true when all their competitors are generating fees doing exactly that—and taking full advantage of the wellness bubble before it pops.

And, as we amply demonstrated in *Why Nobody Believes the Numbers*, vendored wellness is a bubble. There is zero evidence that wellness program vendors control healthcare costs. There is considerable evidence that some of what they do—especially biometric screens that send many people rushing off to the doctor—*increases* costs, and overwhelming evidence that almost all of them completely fabricate their return-on-investment numbers.

Both the zero return from wellness and the hidden costs of screens (each covered later in this book) are widely known among advisors, and yet most of you reading this have been sold or are being sold a vendored wellness program (which usually includes screening).

Why? Because advisors need to propose and implement these programs to make money. An analogy to this situation is residential real estate. During the massive bubble earlier this century, real estate brokers who represented buyers would often advise them to bid higher, for the simple reason that they didn't earn a commission if someone else's client outbid them. Many brokers knew their clients couldn't afford the payments and/or that the price being charged was unsupportable. However, acting on that knowledge—perhaps by advising the client to simply rent a home instead—would have bank-rupted them. So providing the best advice and making the most money were complete opposites in that scenario and provide a classic example of what economists call a "moral hazard."

Later in this chapter is a list of questions that you need to ask of your advisors to make sure that you are getting the best advice. To provide multiple perspectives, we've assembled a panel of brokers and consultants to comment on each of the questions. These are people, who, in our experience, offer a combination of integrity and competence. It's possible your broker fits this bill, too. As mentioned in the introduction, one way to know if yours fits the bill is to answer this question: Did yours tell you about the existence of this book? Like its prequel, *Why Nobody Believes the Numbers*—only more so—*Cracking Health Costs* can and should be very threatening to brokers and consultants who don't.

Just as later chapters will show with hospital reputations, there is zero or even inverse correlation between consulting firm name recognition and actual competence in advisory services. In the same way that our search for Company Sponsored Centers of Excellence led us to lesser known hospitals, our extensive search for the most competent brokers and consultants led us to 10 who primarily serve the middle market. (Four of these individuals, Scott Haas, Mark Kendall, Mike Sammons, and Dr. Dave Rearick, are highlighted elsewhere in this book.)

The reason for this divergence? Very large companies rarely change consulting firms, thereby telegraphing to their consulting firms that they've essentially received tenure. For instance, that large hospital system described in this chapter's first paragraph still uses the same consulting firm that gave it arguably the most self-serving advice in benefits consulting history (which isn't an easy distinction to achieve in that field). Those large firms often implicitly or explicitly also hold out the possibility of their HR client contacts working for them someday as well, which smaller companies can rarely do.

Note that we do not list any affiliations below in order to prevent readers from mistaking our recognition and appreciation of the work, insight, and philosophies of leading individuals for endorsements of the organizations with which these individuals are currently affiliated. Other advisors affiliated with those same organizations may not (or may) share those same attributes.

Members of the Panel

- ◆ Melissa Tobler, her company's national practice leader for health strategies. She has worked with mid-market employers in planning and evaluating employer health and wellness initiatives. She is certified in Critical Outcomes Report Analysis (CORA) from the Disease Management Purchasing Consortium (CORA is the industry's only outcomes measurement certification).
- ◆ Jim Millaway, a CORA-certified benefits consultant with an independent brokerage and consulting firm representing more than 2,500 clients in 48 states. He works directly with self-funded employers as well as physicians and health systems.
- ◆ Aaron Davis, also CORA-certified, the founder and president of an advisory firm that employs both employee benefits experts and healthcare clinicians. Aaron is also the primary author of the www.benebuzz.com blog.
- ◆ Dave Dias, a practice leader and director of one of the country's largest privately held brokerages. He also runs the blog www.insurancethoughtleadership.com.
- ◆ Rick Chelko, the founder and president of a health and welfare benefits consulting firm that serves mid-sized and large

employers. Rick is also copresident of Worldwide Employee Benefits Network (WEB), a professional development and networking group for benefits professionals.

◆ Andy Carr, team leader for wellness services at one of the nation's largest employee-owned brokerage and consulting firms. He has worked with many large employers crafting their health and wellness strategies.

Here are the questions and my take on the answers, supplemented by the panel's views. We asked each of the panelists to comment only on the three questions into which they felt they had the most insight. (Also, if every panelist answered every question, you'd have 48 opinions, including mine, to digest.)

Are your advisor's fees totally transparent?

If you are using a consulting firm, its fees *should* be totally transparent. After all, you are paying the firm directly. You want a guarantee in writing that it isn't accepting any kind of transaction incentives from the vendors it is recommending. Indeed, a good advisor doesn't even recommend in the strictest sense of the word; he or she establishes a process that allows the most appropriate vendor for the situation to win the bid. If your advisor is a licensed broker, he or she is certainly allowed to earn a fee from the vendor, but that fee should be disclosed and, in the case of noncarriers, negotiable where commissions are not governed by statute. And most important, do the math. Those small percentage commissions can add up, and you sense how much time your advisor spends on your account. Advisors should receive fair—but not excessive—compensation for that time.

Carrier commissions can't be rebated to you, by statute. However, you can negotiate an all-in administrative services fee with your carrier that includes a smaller commission than the carrier usually pays—if you and the broker agree to that. As for vendor commissions, see Jim's response. You can always tell when a vendor is offering a fee to push its product because its website has a heading like "Brokers and Consultants" or "Resellers" and code phrases like "we will work with you" or "we will be your partner." Code needs to be used because commissions are too sensitive a subject to discuss explicitly on a website. You might see the website and realize "your" broker is being paid by someone else to sell you stuff.

Another rule of thumb is that there is simply no one-size-fits-all program solution for *anything*—be it a 401(k), payroll, or wellness plan. If 90 percent of your advisor's clients are with certain vendors, there is very likely money being exchanged—and more than likely, it's not transparent. You, therefore, want to ask for a breakdown of percentages of clients with various vendors in any given space to better understand the complexities of market relationships.

Jim Millaway: Fees must be transparent. There is no reason to trust your advisor if he or she is taking bribes behind your back (and yes, they are bribes). Employers can't imagine how many vendors show up at my office. And a large—if not the biggest—part of their product pitch is how much I can expect to earn and how much more they pay than their competitor. If the vendor has to rely on that level of manipulation to move its product or program, what are the chances it really works anyway?

Aaron Davis: As the clients in this scenario, employers technically control the relationship. Yet they oftentimes don't take advantage of that position. I encourage them to conduct their own due diligence and implement a rigorous RFP process for broker or consultant selection ahead of any vendor choices that will ultimately follow the relationship. If they don't, the advisor, if not the broker of record (meaning they get the commission no matter which vendor or carrier is selected), will recommend the vendors they represent—the ones who will pay them a commission.

Andy Carr: You should never feel like you can't ask the broker if he would be getting a commission on the service he is recommending—and if so, how much. Sometimes a commission can make sense for compensating the broker's time, and other times it is just excessive; do the math to discern which. But no matter the case, that commission should never drive a broker's decision about a service for you.

Rick Chelko: Sometimes, a brokerage firm's bottom line is entirely based upon carrier incentives. Even the most well-intentioned broker can't run away from this reality. They start managing this bottom line by subtly manipulating the bidding process (tilting the playing field) to produce an outcome that looks like it better serves the client, but in the end, the process "burns markets," meaning that some vendors won't bid on your business because they know the game is rigged. If your broker is telling you that many carriers won't quote on your business, it may be a sign that the broker has ruined the competitive market for you.

Unfortunately, insurance carriers and other vendors are very adept at rewarding brokers for new business, for keeping business on the books, and for helping them to make it profitable business. For example, one of our large bank clients used a broker to shop its group life plan. The employer got the broker to agree to not take any commission overrides on its account; however, the employer did not know that its business would still have a large impact on the broker's overrides on the rest of its "book."

Does your advisor write massive RFPs to generate the perception that a lot of work is being done?

Long RFPs provide shockingly little value, since there is shockingly little difference among most carriers and vendors in most segments of managed health services. Nonetheless, *Why Nobody Believes the Numbers* excerpted a major benefits consulting firm's disease management RFP for the Commonwealth of Virginia that required 237 cells to be completed with numbers—for just the single section of the RFP on the financial guarantee. These cells served no purpose other than to justify the consulting fees, because only 10 numbers were needed had the consulting firm used the optimal bid configuration. It wasn't just a waste of everyone's time to complete and then evaluate all those cells. It was that somehow the broker never asked for the correct 10 numbers even though he had 237 chances to do so. You'd think he'd be able to get a few of them right, just based on random chance.

Melissa Tobler: Develop your strategic plan, including the objectives and metrics you want to measure, prior to looking for vendors. This allows you to narrow the search to vendors and programs that support the organization's goals, instead of what usually happens: you see an impressive presentation on the latest and greatest—which can be fueled by fees or commissions to the intermediary—and then adopt that product even if it doesn't address your employees' actual needs.

Whether you are procuring carriers or niche vendors, there are probably only about 15 to 25 points of distinction that you need to know about. If you ask a gazillion more questions than that, you'll simply lose focus and slow down the entire process. Remember, these suppliers wouldn't be in business if they couldn't do the simple stuff right.

Jim Millaway: You need to concentrate only on how the vendor can do three things: provide better care, improve employee health, and lower cost —by significant amounts. If an RFP question won't fit into one of those three categories, then it's probably just logistical or of minor relevance. If it's a contractual issue, the threshold for including it in the RFP is that it should be a major contractual term that you want to clarify in advance to avoid misunderstandings during the contracting process itself. An example might be termination for convenience.

Dave Dias: Much of the time there's what I call an "RFP conspiracy" occurring in the background of the RFP process. This occurs in many cases where products and services have already been determined by the broker and his vendors—which means that the RFP is merely camouflage for placing more, and usually unnecessary, product.

Andy Carr: An RFP should not be synonymous with an essay contest. You and your broker should only need this document to do four things: provide the vendor with enough background information to give you a proposal; tell them what is important to you; ask specific questions about those important elements; and give the vendor selection criteria for the winner. It likely doesn't require hundreds of questions or pages to do that.

Does your advisor take other steps of dubious value to make it look like an entire team is necessary for your project, like producing massively detailed work plans, action steps, and so on?

These projects are mostly off-the-shelf. The reams of paper being photocopied are no different from other reams of paper produced for other accounts. And you don't want paper; you want an outcome—specifically, the right vendor or carrier at a competitive price with a few points of customization to meet your needs. Do not confuse activity with results.

Melissa Tobler: If your advisor steps in and says he will do all the work for you when it comes to designing and implementing a health program—don't let 'em! It may initially make your life easier, but it may also lessen the impact of your wellness program. Owning the initiatives is essential to success—and no one really knows your business as well as you do. You can rely on your advisor for resources, guidance, expert advice, and tools to assist in the planning, but take the time to actually plan and implement yourself.

Jim Millaway: I can run all kinds of detailed action plans, benefit strategy timelines, and planning road maps. And while dumping paper on you is the easiest thing for me to do, I am not sure where the value lies in doing so. Imagine if someone from Amazon wanted to meet with you after each purchase to make sure you understood every step of the supply chain. Your first purchase would have probably been your last (and Amazon wouldn't make any money unless it was billing you for that meeting as well your purchase). Amazon gives you a clear understanding of the finished product and a general timeline to go along with it; all you really need is an e-mail with a link to track the package. Likewise, it should not take your broker 15 pages to express what we are working on and when it should be done.

Dave Dias: A concise, one-page Written Service Timeline developed in conjunction with clients clearly communicates expectations and puts employer and advisor on the same page.

Rick Chelko: If your consultant intends to bring staff members to a meeting who don't have specific roles there, have the consultant do so at his or her own expense (not yours). My general rule of thumb: consultants are expensive. They can provide a lot of value, but use them carefully—as if it is your own money.

Does your advisor act as a gatekeeper in a bid process and prevent vendors from talking with you directly?

My co-author Al Lewis often advises buyers (or brokers themselves) in disease management and wellness procurements. He argues that a broker who cuts off direct bidder-employer communication lacks confidence in his mastery of the procurement process. Such a broker is likely afraid—and if he is afraid, it's probably for good reason—that a vendor will make him look bad in a one-on-one conversation with the buyer.

Aaron Davis: Such brokers also lack mastery of the subject matter itself—something that a one-on-one conversation would also reveal. That's why we employ people who have experience designing, implementing, and managing medical management programs. Because they don't have that expertise, brokers are often afraid that they'll be fighting with the carrier for the client's affections. If the client trusts the carrier more than the broker, the broker should find another line of work.

Al weighed in on this question, too. Though he's not a benefits consultant, companies often call him in to fix procurement, contractual, and evaluation messes that consultants and brokers have left behind (sometimes in court)—so he consequently has a few opinions of his own. He notes that the advisor has to manage the process; there can't be multiple uncoordinated phone calls. So Al's solution is to set up a call with the procurer if the vendor requests it (assuming the former agrees to it)—but not participate himself. He also encourages the procurer to allow the losing vendors to call afterward to make comments on the bidding process.

When he is not the buy-side advisor, Al advises vendors, often trying to interpret murky clauses that the benefits consultant has included in the RFP. Frequently, as with some recent Virginia or Vermont RFPs for disease management, the consultant is obviously wrong, but bidders would equally obviously be impolitic to bring that up in discussion. Ironically, in those two cases, the consultant's clauses—mind you, this is a consultant advising the *buyer*—made it almost impossible for the vendor not to show savings, no matter how ineffective the program. This led to state taxpayers paying large sums to a consultant for the privilege of paying large sums to a vendor who would be able to go on vacation and still show significant savings. (After *Why Nobody Believes the Numbers* noted that Vermont's required ROI methodology was the poster child for invalidity, the state's consulting firm doubled down on cluelessness and now includes that Vermont measurement clause in all its RFPs.)

Dave Dias: Transparency must define the entire bid process. Over the years and on many occasions, I have facilitated private calls and meetings between my client and potential vendors. This promotes trust and expedites a potentially clumsy process. The broker/advisor must own the moral weight and leadership of the process for which he or she is responsible, but a broker who controls the process is insecure and perhaps operating with conflicting objectives.

Andy Carr: It's not the broker's place to determine what is important to understand or ask questions; that's your role. You are the one who ultimately has to be happy with and have the relationship with the vendor—so insist on direct contact.

Is your advisor focused on the big picture?

Melissa Tobler: Let's be clear here: the hard work is not choosing a program or vendor. The tough and time-consuming part involves developing a customized strategy. And this is precisely why many advisors don't do this—because it's not as easy as simply changing the client name on an already developed strategy, RFP, or other deliverable that is supposed to look like it took some time to put together. If your advisor is simply looking at plug-and-play options, you're unlikely to see any impact, financial or otherwise.

If your advisor is touting some extra service (like disease management, wellness, smartphone apps, and so on) designed to reduce your number of chronic disease events, does it even know what your number of chronic disease events *is* ?

Most consultants who claim expertise in wellness, disease management, and smart phone apps have no idea what they are doing. If they did, vendors wouldn't be boasting about their fictitious ROIs, because they would know that consultants wouldn't believe them. They will cite risk factors and predictive modeling and outcomes reports, and the importance of hiring them to do reconciliations. But if they don't know how to count events, how on earth can they measure savings? Savings are basically the number of events avoided times the cost of an event. If you don't count events, you can't figure out if you've reduced them and if so, by how many, making it impossible to do that savings calculation.

Aaron Davis: They'll spread fear and sell hope. They'll tell you your diabetics are out of control and need a smart phone app to help control their disease, but try asking them how many heart attacks or other events their diabetics had last year.

Rick Chelko: Beware of the concepts versus the reality of services. One of my favorite examples is an employer that spent $250,000 per year on disease management. It seemed to the employer like the right thing to do, because it had a lot of plan members with chronic conditions. However, in the end, the vendor only truly engaged three plan members in the program—only one of whom was a high cost claimant.

So what is the action step for all of this? First, your embedded long-time consultants aren't adding any value and are charging you a lot of money. So instead of negotiating yet another contract with them, we recommend auctioning off your business. Announce your total requirements and ask for one fee. Expect your spending on consultants or previously hidden brokerage fees to fall by close to half—even if you keep the same consulting firm. Your consultants will likely stop doing unnecessary 15-page work plans, 100-page RFPs, overly detailed but completely invalid outcomes analyses, and—my favorite—site tours of vendors on your nickel. But you probably shouldn't end up with the same consultant if the bids are close. If our research into this market-place showed us anything, it's that some nimble and flexible middle-market firms are far more capable of doing this job than the old-line houses.

But don't take our word for this. Simply ask your consultants the 15 questions listed in the introduction, and see how many they get right.

Chapter 3

It's Time for the Wellness Industry to Admit to Doping

This chapter has two parts. First, we'll show you why you want to erase every piece of misinformation with which the wellness *ignorati* have indoctrinated you. Yes, we know "ignorati" is not a word (yet), but to paraphrase the great philosopher Clarice Starling, there isn't a name for what they are. It's not just that the entire industry apparently played hooky the day the fifth-grade teacher covered arithmetic. It's not even that they refuse to allow data or even proof to disrupt their belief system. It's that they take pride in their ignorance. Al tried to explain to one of them that no reputable behavioral economist thinks you can bribe people with incentives to overcome addictions, and he replied that there was no such thing as behavioral economics. The *ignorati* simply don't believe in facts. This is not to say they are stupid. Quite the opposite: they disbelieve facts because they are smart enough to recognize that facts are their worst nightmare.

Hence they will dispute this proven conclusion: wellness will not reduce your health spending, period.* Next, we'll take a brief look at what wellness *can* do—which, you'll be happy to hear, are a few things. First, it can turn an unpopular increase in employee contribution into a popular way for some employees to feel they are saving money. Second, it can significantly improve the composition of your workforce—not by making a lot of unhealthy people healthy (though a few will benefit), but by creating an environment that makes it easier to recruit and retain healthier people. Third, if done right, it can be an inexpensive way to tell your employees you care about them—and that is an end in itself.

Given the complete innumeracy of the *ignorati*, the (unsurprising) ultimate irony in wellness is that these three places where you can probably expect to see a benefit have never before been identified as major opportunities to find a return.† On the other hand, the one place

---

* If you don't also reach this same conclusion after reading this chapter, I would recommend Al's seminal article in *Health Affairs*, January 16, 2013, that he wrote with Vik Khanna. http://healthaffairs.org/blog/2013/01/16/is-it-time-to-re-examine-workplace-wellness-get-well-quick-schemes/.

† While it is true as of this writing that no one has systematically studied the economic impact of a healthy workplace on recruitment/retention of healthier (read more productive) employees, keep an eye on the website for the Institute for Health and Productivity Management, www.ihpm.org. As of this writing, IHPM is forging ahead in that unexplored arena, and perhaps by the time you read this will have conferences or other materials that advance the issue far beyond the intuitive but speculative comments here.

you absolutely won't see a return—in reduced healthcare costs—has been the focus of most of the savings propaganda.

Part One: Vendored Wellness Programs Do Not, Will Not, and Never Have Reduced Your Health Spending, Period

I know what you're thinking: "Don't hold back, Tom. Tell us how you really feel." Okay, if you insist. Here goes.

If someone has convinced you to put a program in place, you're not alone. Health-contingent wellness programs* have become the Fortune 500's single biggest discretionary healthcare investment. According to the National Business Group on Health, just the annual wellness program participation incentives alone exceed $521 per employee. Repeat: that is for incentives alone. It doesn't even include the cost of the actual program.

And this isn't limited to the Fortune 500. Wellness savings assumptions are so widely accepted that the Affordable Care Act includes taxpayer-financed wellness incentives for small businesses. Wellness supporters cite peer-reviewed literature that cites average reductions of 25 percent in health spending[1] (yielding returns on investment exceeding 3 to 1 in health cost savings[2]) to justify this spending.

We're here to tell you that, peer-reviewed or not, all those savings estimates and ROIs are indeed—to quote the immortal word of the great philosopher U.S. Vice President Joe Biden—malarkey. How do we know? Because these corporate, governmental, and peer-reviewed endorsements of wellness programs to reduce healthcare spending directly contradict both simple arithmetic and insurance marketplace behavior, that's how.

So who's right—the marketplace and the arithmetic or the pundits, academicians, and government? As is often the case when third parties and the government try to outthink the market, the market wins. The sophisticated segment—insurers who eat, sleep, and drink medical

---

* The ACA distinguishes "health-contingent" programs, involving health risk assessments and screens, from "participatory" wellness programs, which involve creating a culture of wellness by helping people to improve their health. We are fans of the latter, but as an employer you shouldn't need a law to identify a culture of wellness as a good thing.

Why Are You Paying People to Lie to You?

As the *Wall Street Journal* elegantly noted (February 18, 2013), many people lie to their doctors even though they are paying their doctors, and those lies might have health consequences. Why wouldn't even more people lie on an HRA when those lies have essentially no health consequences and when they aren't quite sure that the boss won't see their answers?

Moreover, you are *paying* them to lie to you. The reason your employees need incentives to complete HRAs is because their innate value is so trivial that almost nobody would bother to complete one without getting paid to do so. (Those who want to complete them can find them free, online and with no concerns, however misguided they might be, about privacy.)

Yet somehow this seemingly obvious observation has eluded many an HR department. Folks in HR would no doubt be quite surprised if, when they were about to pay for a pound of dried seaweed at checkout, the cashier said: "Seaweed is good for you, so you don't have to pay for it. In fact, I'll even pay you to take some home." People with no interest in seaweed (like me) might simply fetch some and then throw it out (like I would do), just to collect the incentive payment. People might also pretend they ate it, if they thought that mattered to the HR department.

Ridiculous? Perhaps, but that incentive is essentially what you are offering your employees to complete an HRA . . . and I'd bet that's their likely reaction.So the irony is paying people to create a culture of health instead creates a culture of deceit.

spending—finds the math to be both straightforward and compelling. As a result, they don't incentivize wellness for fully insured policyholders. Yet the employer segment—HR departments that have many other responsibilities and are not staffed by biostatisticians and instead rely on consultants—does.

It's easy to explain the dichotomy. In the employer segment we find a case study in market breakdown. First, a major information asymmetry exists because the human resources executives who purchase these programs aren't trained to identify biostatistical outcomes measurement fallacies. Second, they rely upon benefits consultants to do so—the very people who make a great deal of money procuring and evaluating these programs. This creates quite the moral hazard. (See Chapter 2, "Does Your Broker or Consultant Have Your Back?")

Finally, so-called actuarial validations of wellness savings are often financed by the entities that want to justify their results. As *Why Nobody Believes the Numbers* demonstrates with North Carolina Medicaid, even the field's highest-priced actuarial self-validations are full of impossible and contradictory findings. Once they got caught, the actuaries retracted their major finding. Perhaps the least valid validation is a vendor highlighted in *Why Nobody Believes the Numbers* claiming an 85 percent reduction in total cost even though the *New England Journal of Medicine* shows 0 percent. Its intervention, according to its website, isn't just validated but rather is "strongly validated," perhaps on the theory that regular validation is for sissies. So the correlation is clear: the stronger the validation language, the less valid the outcome.

Many vendors who haven't paid somebody to lie on their behalf will say their outcomes or ROI are "documented." Somehow vendors feel that word should impress people, perhaps because it contains so many syllables and/or perhaps because the word "document" reminds people of seeing the original Declaration of Independence on their eighth-grade trip, but "documented" is defined on dictionary.com as "any written item, as in a book, article, or letter." So "documentation" only means that the vendor's outcomes are jotted down on a piece of paper somewhere.

Bottom line: your counterparts in other self-insured employers are wrong, and the insurance companies are right. Valid measurement is the wellness industry's Kryptonite. What follows are some examples of all the techniques they use to show savings, techniques so far removed from validity that light leaving validity wouldn't even reach them for several seconds. The reason that the health insurance industry wants nothing to do with get well quick programs that your counterparts at other companies embrace is that these programs' savings figures are built on impossible arithmetic, nonexistent data, invalid study designs, denial of both common sense and medical literature, and what a lexicographer might term "lies."

IMPOSSIBLE ARITHMETIC

First, consider the arithmetic. Let's start out with the mathematical impossibility of the aforementioned 25 percent average savings claimed in the *American Journal of Health Promotion*. What that journal doesn't mention is that this is impossible, because only about 7 percent of your total spending—at the very most—pays for medical events like heart attacks that are preventable through wellness. Yes, 7 percent. Essentially your whole corporate healthcare strategy has been turned upside down to chase 7 percent of your spending. Let's say you reduce that 7 percent by a tenth, which is a realistic goal. That's . . . hmmm . . . my math is a little rusty but I get a 0.7 percent reduction in your total spending. And for that you're paying each employee $521 in incentives, plus another few hundred dollars in program costs, plus more trips to the doctor?

Cracking Health Costs' mantra: don't take my word for it. Do the math. *Why Nobody Believes the Numbers* shows how, step by step. Yes, it's logical that better health habits will generate less health spending, and they do—*after* your employees retire. The wellness-sensitive medical event rate in your retired population is about 10 times the rate in your population today. In other words, all this expense and aggravation you are undertaking today won't help you, but it will help Medicare keep *its* cost down. A cynic might say the government has effectively privatized the cost of public health, while keeping most of the benefits for itself.

The *ignorati* don't mention that only 7 percent of your spending pays for wellness-sensitive medical events because it's not traditional in wellness to track wellness-sensitive events. The tradition is to claim credit for everything that improves among participants. It's a little like a drug company saying: "We don't care what disease you had. If you got better it was because of our drug." Nor does the impossibility of saving 25 percent when only 7 percent is even theoretically available to be saved bother them. For wellness *ignorati*, immutable rules of arithmetic are just a bump in the road. (Your consultants encourage this. If wellness is a virus attacking the business community's financial health, the benefits consulting industry is Typhoid Mary.)

I say "even theoretically" because many of those events take place in people who are beyond needing to eat more broccoli. The impact of what Chapter 2's Melissa Tobler calls "chronic disease runout" means that even a perfect wellness program can't reverse disease progression in people who have already experienced complications of chronic disease. They will continue to deteriorate, albeit perhaps at a slower pace than otherwise. And these are the ones who end up in the hospital.

Also many employees won't be identified as at-risk, many at-risk employees won't participate, and many participants won't succeed.

Further, if you want to reduce heart attacks, strokes, and wellness-sensitive cancers in your company through wellness programs, you'll also need to hire a vendor to figure out how to reverse aging and modify your workers' genetics, since both aging and genetics are root causes of or major contributors to those and countless other diseases. (While I doubt any vendors are addressing these two issues just yet, I'm sure they'll report terrific outcomes when they do.)

We're not the only people to notice this mathematical impossibility. The health insurance industry has no doubt done the same arithmetic. We know this, because not one single publicly held company in the business of controlling medical care expenses actually provides financial incentives for *their own* commercially insured members to complete HRAs and talk to coaches—despite the fact that the widely cited peer-reviewed literature mentioned above suggests that doing so could multiply their profits. (Many offer HRAs and coaching, and if a member wants to participate—great. But they don't bribe their members to say they are participating, even though they are more than happy to sell programs to help you do that with your employees. Some do offer small discounts for people willing to go to the gym 12 times a month, a policy which—even in the very likely event that it doesn't attract new users—makes great actuarial sense for retaining the healthy members they want to retain.)

NONEXISTENT DATA AND INVALID STUDY DESIGNS

Next, consider the data: Despite needing massive reductions in wellness-sensitive medical events (such as heart attacks) to justify alleged savings/ROIs and pay for the incentives, no vendor or consultant has ever measured employer-wide reductions in wellness-sensitive medical events. Nor has any vendor or consultant ever tracked these events over time at a workplace, or—until Al, the Institute for Health and

Productivity Management, and others formed an intercompany task force to do so in 2013—even *made a list* of wellness-sensitive medical events. (By contrast, there are long-established lists of medical events that both disease management and primary care can potentially prevent.)

Vendor study designs almost invariably compare motivated wellness program participants to nonmotivated nonparticipants. So despite the fact that wellness success only works for people who are motivated, this control methodology puts all the motivated people in the study group. It's therefore no surprise that a presentation by Health Fitness Corporation and Eastman Chemical Company showed that medical spending for Eastman's would-be participants fell 9 percent relative to nonparticipants in the first year of separating the groups. However, that 9 percent relative improvement couldn't have been due to the program, because the groups were separated *12 months before the program even started*. Nonetheless, the companies credited the program for that 9 percent that happened before the program started. Another vendor website shows similar savings—$350 per year (about 8 percent of health spending)—that could be achieved for every participant who did not reduce risk factors, just by being a participant.

DENIALS OF COMMON SENSE AND THE MEDICAL LITERATURE

Pack-a-day smokers in most states could save about $2,500 a year by quitting, creating a tremendous economic incentive—about $100,000 over 40 years—to quit. Yet, if we're to believe vendor claims instead of common sense, a large number of smokers have quit when offered a few hundred bucks and nicotine patches. (The health reform law now allows penalties for smokers into the four figures; that should make a difference in smoking rates.)

The medical literature does not contain one shred of evidence that preventive physician visits improve health. In fact, it skews the other way. See Jane Brody's January 21, 2013, *New York Times* "Personal Health" column or the previously cited article "Think Prevention Will Save Money? Think Again" by Sharon Begley (Reuters, January 29, 2013) for lay views. Nonetheless, the follow-up advice from health risk assessments almost invariably recommends visiting the doctor more (on your nickel).

LIES

You know that old joke: "How can you tell if a lawyer is lying?" Answer: His lips move.

Well, here's how you can tell when vendor savings claims are invalid: the vendor is claiming savings. And when it comes to claiming savings, many companies won't stop at nothing. That is not a misprint. One can only reduce any healthcare expense number (or any other number) to nothing, meaning by only 100 percent, tops. Yet somehow, one wellness vendor website claims that program participants are 230 percent less likely to incur disability expenses than nonparticipants; another claims a 300 percent reduction in absenteeism; and a third boasts a 340 percent reduction in health spending.[*]

One of my favorites is a vendor whose website claims a very precise and extremely massive 14.3-to-1 ROI on their health risk assessment alone. This, despite the fact that HRAs are anonymous and voluntary, not tied to claims in any way, and—here's a shocker—sometimes respondents don't tell the truth. And if you find a health risk that needs to be addressed, you generally spend money to do so when you follow up. A perfect example of this would be my very own collaborator, Al Lewis. Although he was deemed low-risk, Al's HRA report suggested 17 exams and tests—about $500 worth—including a PSA test for prostate cancer, even though those are no longer recommended by the Centers for Disease Control (CDC) and a meningitis vaccine, perhaps on the off-chance he was about to visit Africa, one of the few instances in which the CDC recommends such a vaccine. Al also checked off "7 or more" prescription drugs even though he listed no diagnoses, setting up the HRA report to make the obvious cost-saving and quality-improving observation that his drugs and diagnoses were totally out of whack and that he should consult a physician. The report he was given missed that improvement opportunity altogether.

---

[*] Nor is this innumeracy confined to wellness. In a study on patient-centered medical homes, the Institute for Healthcare Improvement reported a "350 percent decline" in patient waiting times. I guess that means that $3\frac{1}{2}$ hours before your appointment, a limo comes to your door and whisks you into the doctor's office. And don't leave out our POTUS, who once publicly announced, to resounding applause, that the Affordable Care Act would "reduce premiums by 3,000 percent." True, Governor Romney's numbers didn't add up, either, but at least he was aware you couldn't reduce a number by more than 100 percent. No matter how many people you lay off.

Bottom line: the HRA report proposed 17 tests and exams, of which 15 were likely useless or redundant and 2 completely wrong . . . and totally missed the one health issue it should have noted. And this is one of the country's largest wellness vendors. This vendor has plenty of company in the inappropriateness category. Another major wellness vendor recommends lung CT scans for nonsmokers, with no mention of the overwhelming likelihood that a "spot" would be a false-positive.

Even the iconic Safeway story of achieving a zero medical inflation trend through wellness—the inspiration for the wellness provisions in the Affordable Care Act—has one very significant flaw: it's made up. *The Washington Post* (January 16, 2010) observed that Safeway's zero medical cost trend predated its wellness initiative by several years.

2013 has been a banner year for lies and misrepresentations. One vendor breathlessly announced how much weight was lost by program participants who lost weight, without noting the percentage that actually lost weight at all. Another boasted "85 percent of people's risk factors either improved or stayed the same," creating a massive reduction in cost. However, a close look at that vendor's own report— not challenging the report's assumptions, mind you, simply reading the report's results—reveals that only 20 percent improved while 65 percent stayed the same and the other 15 percent deteriorated. Hence it would have been equally valid to say: "80 percent of people either failed to improve or got worse." The latter would have undermined the vendor's massive cost savings claims, though. In fact, dividing their cost savings by the net number of people whose risks went down yields almost $20,000 in savings per person.

Essentially, every wellness study showing substantial savings and/or risk factor reduction is obviously wrong—as more and more of your peers are learning. However, the *ignorati* live in a parallel universe, where they are the Mikeys of phony outcomes reports.[*] You can subscribe to the oxymoronically named Wellness Smartbrief from America's Health Insurance Plans (AHIP) to get daily examples. For instance, as I write this today (February 18, 2013), the AHIP Smartbrief

---

[*] If you're under 45, that allusion requires a brief explanation. It's a reference to an iconic cereal commercial where Mikey would eat anything. Likewise, most benefits consultants and brokers will believe any outcomes report, and support the findings to their client.

linked to an article in the *Columbian* describing a $3 million program for 157 Clark County (Washington) law enforcement officers with "metabolic syndrome" (a recently coined term for someone who may develop diabetes or heart disease). The program sponsors said the ROI on this type of program was 10 to 1. But neither the AHIP Smartbrief editor nor the program sponsor divided the $30,000,000 alleged savings claimed by the 157 officers with metabolic syndrome. Those savings worked out to about $190,000 in savings per person, the large majority of whom didn't even have diagnosed diabetes or heart disease yet. And of course, $190,000 per person is vastly more than Clark County even spends on healthcare.

And of course, as is traditional in the wellness field, no one actually measured whether wellness-sensitive medical events declined at all. Not that it matters, because in a population that size there would be so few such events that even a valid measurement technique would be subject to a lot of random variation.

Speaking of eating better, I have a nurse friend who spends a disproportionate share of her day in inpatient nutritional counseling. Yet as a hospital employee, she is eligible for incentives for attending nutrition classes. However, since she could teach the course, she simply sits in the back of the room, reading a novel and collecting her windfall.

Al and I aren't the only ones who recognize that these outcomes are pure fantasy. Even some wellness vendors themselves are willing to tell the truth about their ROIs and the industry's. They are listed on Al's website (www.dismgmt.com) under "Gold Standard" and kudos to them for their integrity. Hopefully the market will reward companies for integrity at some future point, but for now made-up ROIs, the higher the better, rule the day. One enterprising company, having struck out on reducing actual claims costs, purports to earn 17-to-1 ROIs by reducing "undetected claims costs." I have no idea what those are, but this vendor usually reduces them by a multiple of actual total claims costs.

In addition to these individual head-scratchers, perhaps the entire wellness storyline should be questioned before $521 per employee gets spent on incentives alone. If so many employers are having so much success in wellness, then why is obesity climbing, and why has the decline in smoking rates stalled out? Why does our population health status continue to deteriorate? In brief, if these programs are so good, why are the numbers that matter so bad?

The lessons from all of this? Whereas the *ignorati* think you can keep large numbers of people out of hospitals by attaching pedometers to them, I am more skeptical. And I've actually run a health benefit as opposed to claiming expertise on health spending from afar. It's like Al says: "Following my divorce, I noticed that most of the childless women I dated were outspoken experts on how I should raise my children while the actual moms I dated rarely offered me any advice, even when I solicited it."

The action plan is simple. Employers should reallocate wellness dollars from get-well-quick vendor schemes into the much more challenging—but ultimately more rewarding—task of creating a culture of wellness, a workplace that can attract and retain healthy people. And the next section will show you exactly how to do this.

Before we move on, you might be thinking, "I'd like to see the wellness industry's rebuttal of these observations." Okay, if you insist. Since the *ignorati* all read the same journals, support one another on the same LinkedIn groups, and congregate at same conferences like monarch butterflies of innumeracy, it's easy to identify the belly of their beast: the self-described "premier resource for wellness information," the Wellness Council of America (www.WELCOA.org). The first piece of wellness information that caught my eye—which Al has helpfully cut-and-pasted for his own website to memorialize it in case WELCOA misplaces its own copy—is that WELCOA was founded by none other than the world-renowned inventor of the all-you-can-eat self-serve restaurant, Warren Buffet. We suspect they meant Warren Buffett, but as I'm sure you know, it is quite common for organizations to misspell the name of their founder on their corporate information page, particularly when it's (1) one of those long phonetically challenging names of (2) someone no one has heard of.

But not to worry. I'm sure all their other premier resources are accurate, where "premier resource" is defined as "anything related to the topic of wellness that supports their viewpoint." Meaning, if you're looking for a rebuttal, you're wasting your time. There is no rebuttal because to rebut something one needs to acknowledge its existence. This organization has chosen to highlight and link to every "premier resource" of wellness ROI information except Al's best-selling book on the topic and the wellness journal article with the most citations in 2013 (Al's co-authored January article in *Health Affairs*[3]). As they say in Argentina, the wellness industry has disappeared Al, which flatters him no end.[*]

Nor is WELCOA the exception when it comes to nonrebuttals. Several of the vendors profiled above, when asked by that (very same) Reuters health reporter Sharon Begley (in an article published April 29, 2013) to defend their outcomes claims, refused to comment—sort of the analytical equivalent of the perp walk. Just to be clear, it's not like Ms. Begley retained Julian Assange or Rupert Murdoch to hack into their e-mails. What the vendors were refusing to comment on were *their own marketing materials*.

The bottom line? There is an utter lack of metrics and, really, an utter lack of thought. We're now more at a herd mentality.

Yes, I really shouldn't be making such inflammatory statements. The good news is, I don't have to. That's a direct quote (*Business Week*, May 22, 2013) from a major wellness supporter, the manager of benefits at the Society for Human Resource Management. Apparently, he didn't get the memo that candor and wellness don't mix.

Part Two: The Actual Value of Wellness

You can't purchase a culture of wellness with individual incentives. Your company must invest in its workplace. As such, there are at least three undeniable ways to profitably deploy a wellness program. One is tactical, one strategic, and one morale-building. Naturally, none has anything to do with any aspect of the vendored get-well-quick programs.

We'll begin with an easy tactic. Suppose you want to raise your annual deductible or contribution or anything else that increases employee share of spending. Let's say that you'd specifically like to raise the monthly contribution from $100 to $110. Of course, one obvious way to do that is simply to raise the monthly contribution from $100 to $110. You didn't need to buy a book to tell you that. So *Cracking Health Costs* will tell you this: a much better way to achieve that increase is to *announce* that you are raising the monthly

---

[*] In all fairness, not every wellness "premier resource" filters out facts. The aforementioned Institute for Health and Productivity Management would be the exception to that rule.

contribution to $130. However, in the same announcement, let employees know that their contribution will stay the same—at $100—if they do something that has wellness value.* Experience suggests that about two-thirds of people will opt for the "something" in order to get that $30 a month savings. So you achieve your goal of raising the monthly contribution an average of $10, but with several added advantages:

1. The increase is optional. If people really want to keep their monthly contribution at $100, they can.
2. You've created an incentive without paying for one.
3. You've let your employees know that patrolling their health is an important enough goal that you will subsidize it.
4. You've taken a step toward the ultimate goal below, which is making your organization more attractive for people who are interested in their health.
5. And there is always the chance, however slim, that this "something of wellness value" will prevent a medical event.

This tactic means wellness is really just a cover for a financial decision to raise the employee share of health spending. But there is also a strategic pony in the tactical wellness pile: creating a culture of wellness probably does improve the bottom line. Not by paying a vendor to hire coaches, paying your employees to promise to eat more broccoli, or by trying to turn your obese smokers into triathletes—but by making your organization more attractive to healthy people in the first place. Focusing on retention and recruitment is a much easier way to create a wellness culture than trying to change the inherent nature of the people in your company now. (Recall the analogy from the first chapter about trying to turn Greek workers into German workers.) Chapter 10 describes well-being as a tangible way to create more of a culture of wellness.

The healthcare benefit itself—which is what this book is about—has little to do with creating a culture of wellness. However, if your

---

* I don't like to dictate the specifics, and even if I did, there aren't many specifics to dictate since most of this stuff doesn't work. However, I would recommend a requirement of a "commitment contract," as described on www.Stickk.com, in which people set their own goal and put that $360/year at risk for achieving it, so the motivation is intrinsic and the skin in the game is real.

company is small enough, the same people who administer the health benefit run all of human resources, as well. And the human resources department, more than any other, sets the tone for a wellness culture. Yes, I am perfectly familiar with the cliché that a wellness culture starts at the top. It should. But the people at the top probably have more important issues on their plate—like, for example, running the company. Yes, I've seen the studies that wellness vendors have published, claiming that CEOs list wellness programs as a "major strategic imperative." But I suspect Staples and Office Depot put out studies listing office supplies as a major strategic imperative, too.

The fact remains that in most companies, it's up to HR to organize the sports teams and the field day, and to find the money for the on-site fitness center. The other place you'd like to intervene is in the cafeteria, where you can subsidize healthier choices and maybe even "tax" unhealthier ones. However, the cafeteria usually reports through facilities. I don't know the last time you interacted with the guys (and they are generally guys) in facilities, but these are generally not people for whom tofu is a huge priority. Also, cafeteria contractors are paid per meal, the idea being to incentivize them to encourage employees to stay on-site to eat. So they serve what's popular, not what's healthy. Therefore, wresting responsibility for the cafeteria from facilities would by itself be a good step forward. A CEO who wants to start a wellness culture at the top should be willing to take this one step to prove it.

For instance, what if you made your cafeteria vendor source some ingredients from local farmers or Whole Foods, and those items could be clearly labeled as containing these healthy ingredients from recognizable suppliers, sort of like "Intel Inside"? Next, you would reallocate some of your incentive budget toward subsidizing those items, to make them economically as well as gastronomically attractive. Imagine the morale and retention impact on some of your workforce—for the most part that "some" would be the ones you wanted to keep, in order to kindle your culture of wellness.

Beware, though, that if *all* the food is too healthful, people will eat elsewhere, probably at a fast-food place. In this case, you'd lose out both in nutrition and the whole point of the cafeteria, which is to keep people on-site. A good meal planner can solve for that, and hence the words "subsidize" and "tax" in the previous paragraphs. The idea is not to dictate but rather to encourage smart dietary choices.

The *ignorati* are wrong on so many counts that you may notice I'm finding it hard to shut up. Even this list of culture-improving initiatives needs serious qualification. The idea of upgrading the cafeteria and installing fitness facilities reflects a headquarters-centric view of the world. Our recommendations, then, would apply only to the central corporate facility, major plants/call centers, universities, municipalities, hospitals, investment banks, and the like. But what about the large number of major companies with distributed operations, like chain or franchise operations (stores, commercial banks, service stations, hotels, restaurants, day care centers)? Construction companies? Delivery companies? Transportation companies? And what about salespeople and service people who may visit headquarters only a couple of times a year? And what about spouses and dependents—people who may never visit the workplace but whose healthcare costs are still your responsibility?

The vast majority of standalone companies or facilities are simply too small to do these things. Many don't even have cafeterias and exert very little influence over the building manager who might. (Some office buildings do have fitness centers, but they are usually already free.) So the bottom line is, notwithstanding the fuzzy math of the *ignorati*, even wellness programs that work would be of dubious value at many U.S. workplaces. By contrast, health spending is relevant for all of the United States' self-insured companies of any size. That's precisely why this book focuses on that topic.

And while we're speaking of naiveté on the part of the *ignorati*—let me put one more nail in the Safeway coffin. It's not just that its much-revered wellness program didn't exist at the time of the company's zero trend. When Safeway finally did start wellness, its trend spiked. And the program only applied to the company's headquarters staff and other management staff anyway—about 7.5 percent or so of the workforce—as Safeway would clearly fit the category of distributed operations. But don't just take my word for this. Go into any Safeway and ask any employee to show you the fitness facility.

To conclude this chapter on a high note, I did start by saying there were three major advantages to wellness, and I've only noted two. The third is showing your employees you care about them. Many initiatives foster that feeling, and wellness is one of them—but only if you do it in a high-profile, visible way. Paying your employees to complete anonymous forms and have blood drawn is not one of those ways. Sure, your employees will love getting checks for lying anonymously about whether they floss, but they'll also think you're pretty clueless for actually giving them those checks. How's that for ending on a high note?

Okay, I see your point. Let me try again to hit that high note. Even if you don't have a cafeteria there is plenty you can do. Redirect the $521 per person you are saving on worthless incentives to upgrade common areas used by employees, sponsor sports teams and make any other visible work environment improvements you can think of that tell your employees you care about them. At the top of your list should be cleaning the restrooms more often. No employee of any company has ever complained to management that the restrooms were too clean.

That is sure to be a hit, and being a hit with employees matters more than finding a few people who might get sick someday in the future. Think of it this way: If you were leading an army into battle, which would you rather have, troops with high morale or troops with low cholesterol?

Chapter 4

This Is Your Health Benefit on Drugs

L ike Caesar wrote about Gaul, this chapter is divided into three parts, following a brief history. Unlike Caesar, though, we're the ones being conquered. Not by legions on horseback, which would be much easier to defeat, but rather by pharmacy benefit managers (PBMs). That's the subject of the first and second parts. The third part has a bit of good news, some ways to save money despite the PBMs.

First, a little history. In the late 1980s, nascent pharmacy benefit management (PBM) companies started convincing employers that paying them money could reduce their overall costs. This theme was introduced at the beginning of *Cracking Health Costs*—that entire industries of intermediaries have sprung up to convince you that the key to spending less is to spend more.

And maybe that was originally true with PBMs and could possibly still be, but most employers will never know how much value they truly add (if any), because you simply can't find anything less transparent than a PBM contract. What fun would it be for PBMs to simply use their purchasing power to procure low prices? Instead PBMs have created convoluted administrative fee, shared-rebate, formulary, and "implementation fee" schemes that even the savviest employer has only the minutest chance of deciphering.

Did you ever notice that the PBM's fastest penetration years coincided with the fastest growth in the prescription drug cost trend? In all fairness this was partly coincidence. Claritin, a drug whose merits may not have earned it sufficient respect from physicians left to their own judgment, began advertising directly to consumers. Its remarkable success (more remarkable because it offered very little incremental benefit in allergy relief over over-the-counter formulations) spawned others, and it wasn't long before patients would make doctor appointments just to demand pills of various colors (if the name itself wasn't mentioned on the air, no laundry list of side effects needed to be disclosed).

Facing little cost disadvantage at the pick-up window, why would consumers even consider one of the proven older medications when they could instead swallow the exact same pill used by attractive actors and actresses frolicking in a flower-filled meadow? From the physician's perspective, hey, it wasn't their money. Plus, the patient is a customer who could go elsewhere, so why not just give 'em the gosh-darn pill rather than get into a long discussion, especially with six other patients getting fidgety in the waiting room because they've already read the magazines and, hence, have already learned that Iraq invaded Kuwait.

Ultimately—and it took much longer than it should have giving the obviousness of the innovation—PBMs implemented multitiered systems so that users would pay more for drugs they saw on TV and less for generics. Multiple tiers can now be counted as a health benefits success story: generic substitution hits new highs every year, and nonspecialty drugs (more on specialty medications usually used for rare conditions later) as a percentage of health spending has declined.

So that worked, but if you think your PBM is working for you, think again. They're working for themselves, just like you and me and everybody else, of course. Only apparently—unless you are Mark Zuckerberg—more successfully: a dollar invested in one of those companies in 1992 would be worth about $270 today. The most opaque pricing in all of healthcare gives them the opportunity to rip you off many different ways.

I: Striking Back at the PBM Empire

Scott Haas of Wells Fargo Insurance Services is a member of a PBM consulting practice that we believe to be perhaps the country's leading experts on negotiating with these people. He lists a few examples of how they work the system.

Because the majority of PBM contracts prohibit pharmacies from talking to employers, the PBMs can increase their "spread" (what you pay them less what they pay the suppliers) without disclosing their piece of your pie.

The contract between you and a PBM establishes your price, but this price you pay is only loosely related to what the PBM pays to the dispensing pharmacy. This two-independent-contract structure allows the PBMs to "keep the change." As Morningstar wrote about the Express Scripts merger with Medco, the combined company can "use [its] newfound scale to pressure suppliers." The comment does not go on to say: "Unfortunately, their margins won't change because they'll be passing the savings on to employers."

Average Wholesale Price (AWP) discount for generic drugs doesn't matter.

PBMs typically try to price generics to you on an AWP basis. AWP works well (and at all) only for what it was invented to do: to set a price for brand-name patented sole-source drugs that is fair and transparent to the buyer. However, PBMs also use AWP for *exactly the opposite case*—to set a price for non-brand-name nonpatented non-sole-source drugs, three descriptors that more than coincidentally apply to generic drugs . . . and more than coincidentally explain why PBMs want to keep using AWP even when the rationale makes no sense.

Allowing generic drugs to be priced to you this way means all the supplier and pharmacy negotiation benefits go to the PBM. And one generic competitor could underprice the contractual AWP to the PBM without any advantage realized by the PBM being passed on to you. We aren't just talking fractions of a penny, either, as the graph in Figure 4.1 shows.

Corollary: PBMs can tell you that their pricing is "transparent" or "pass-through," but it may not be.

Transparency and pass-through pricing are commonly utilized terms by PBMs to assure clients that they are getting good pricing, but are usually used in conjunction with AWP, which, of course, is

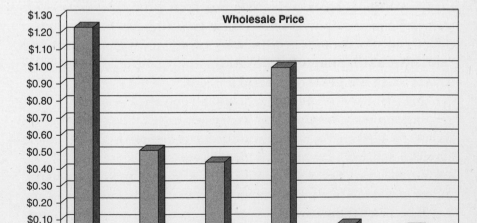

Lisinopril 10mg Tab
Six manufacturers, package size = 90 or 100 units

FIGURE 4.1   Generic Pricing: What Does AWP-70 Percent Mean?

irrelevant if not contraindicated for generics, as they well know. In other words, just taking the word of a PBM salesperson that a transparent or pass-through model PBM is a better deal will serve no value unless your broker/consultant has a clue as to how to truly evaluate the actual drug cost. Unfortunately, very few do.

Mail-order programs frequently cost more.

The premise of mail-order pharmacy is to provide better pricing for the drugs it dispenses. Unfortunately, often the lower employee copay wipes out the savings. And sometimes there is no savings to be wiped out because the mail-order pharmacy is able to create its own (high) AWP by repackaging the drugs it dispenses. This allows the mail-order pharmacy to show a greater stated discount from AWP for mail order than you receive for prescriptions through pharmacies, while at the same time you are actually paying a higher price.

One other unappreciated factor in mail order: Because of the larger volumes dispensed in 90-day versus 30-day prescriptions, mail-order programs historically have experienced more medication wastage, as well.

A $0.00 PBM administration fee may not be a good deal.

While a low-cost or no-cost administrative fee sounds good, this arrangement usually means you're getting ripped off. Administrative fees are dwarfed by the cost reduction achieved through optimal pricing. Often, $10 to $15 per claim is left on the table due to failure to understand the "spread" concept previously described, because you are overnegotiating the administrative fee due to its greater visibility.

The rebate is the ultimate nonopaque component of pricing and is increasingly a distraction.

In just about everything you do in life, you see a price, you pay it, and you're done. Only in PBMs are the prices not the prices. You get rebates for keeping your people on formulary in categories where there is only a choice of brand drugs with no generics. A rebate is visible and it's nice to get a check in the mail, but it's like a tax refund in that it only indicates you may have overpaid in the first place. And with increasing generic substitution, the concept of the preferred formulary is diminishing. Similar to administrative fees, focusing on rebate yield and not on actual pricing might trick you into allowing pricing that costs you much more, on balance, than the rebate check might suggest. If you get a fat rebate check you are maximizing the wrong variable. It's not much of a stretch to say, the larger the rebate check the more you are being snookered.

Also, many PBMs offer to pay you implementation fees to offset legitimate expenses you may incur as you change from one PBM to another. Ever wondered where that windfall is coming from? See "spread pricing," earlier.

To clarify all of these opacities and get you a deal, what exactly are your consultants doing? They're employing the same strategy they are using to prevent your wellness vendor from making up outcomes. I call it the *Seinfeld* strategy: nothing.

Here's how you can be sure I'm right: By far the most important figure to know for negotiating purposes—the only one that cuts through all this clutter—is the spread, the revenue per prescription being siphoned off by your PBM. If your consultants don't know this figure, the most important figure in the whole PBM equation (they don't), and/or it isn't less than $6 per prescription (it isn't), then fire them and retain a firm like Wells Fargo Insurance Services that does, or hope your boss isn't reading this book.

II: Specialty Medications: The Bad News and the Bad News . . . and the Bad News and the Bad News

First, the bad news. It won't be long before 1 to 2 percent of your employees account for half your drug spend, as biologically engineered specialty medications will soon comprise most of the 50 top medications based on total cost. The high annual cost per user easily trumps the small number of users. For instance, it only takes one person with cystic fibrosis treated with medications such as $800-plus per day Kalydeco to explode your cost trend.

Next, the bad news. This will only get worse. Over half the medications currently in the R&D pipeline are specialty medications.

And now for some bad news. There is not much you can do to control the price. However, our resident expert, Mike Sammons of Quest Analytics, has three ideas. To begin with, don't let your employees regularly get these medications from the corner drugstore—insist on use of a specialty pharmacy. Specialty pharmacies provide a better deal since they are set up specifically to deliver these drugs and support the users. Specialty pharmacies employ highly trained pharmacists and nurses who provide individualized case management that is specific to the type of medication being used. They stay in frequent contact with the patient and the treating physician to assure that barriers to optimal clinical outcomes are immediately addressed. They become the trusted confidants for the patient and their family. They also say they prevent waste by monitoring the patient's medication inventory to assure that refills are only sent when needed. Of course, they also make more money the more drugs get purchased, so you still have to keep an eye on them.

The specialty pharmacy requirement can cause extreme frustration when employees visit the local retail pharmacy to obtain their medication. It is therefore best to allow at least one fill and possibly one refill of the medication at the retail pharmacy as this avoids frustrating delays in treatment. With the first retail fill, and the refill if allowed, the pharmacist should be electronically alerted by the PBM to advise the patient of the requirement to use the specialty pharmacy for refills and provide the patient with the telephone number of the specialty pharmacy.

Finally, the good news, which is that this is the last piece of bad news. At this point you won't be surprised to hear this, but your PBMs are ripping you off. This time it's because there is not a bright-line distinction between regular and specialty drugs, particularly as specialty drugs, which historically have required injection or even refrigeration, increasing become available in oral form. Specialty drugs generally are not covered by the rebate or other contractual pricing provisions, so the more drugs PBMs are able to classify as specialty, the more money they make off you.

Your consultants, of course, are blissfully unaware of this, just like they are of the PBM spreads noted previously, rampant wellness mismeasurement noted in the last chapter, and just about everything else in *Cracking Health Costs*. We don't know what they do with their time, but we do know what they don't do with their time, which is use it wisely. At least on your behalf. (They seem to do fine for themselves.)

So what can you do? Well, in addition to insisting on a specialty pharmacy and recontracting to tighten definitions of "specialty," not much. If you are a university—especially one with some kind of clinical training program, whether medical school, nursing school, or any allied health profession—you may be able to take advantage of a quirk in the law to get the price otherwise reserved for hospitals. Check with Mike Sammons on that—this is his schtick.

III: Regular Prescription Drugs

Most consumers walk away with prescriptions without ever knowing the true costs paid by their employer or, for that matter, almost anything else of relevance about that prescription, like whether there is an OTC equivalent. Consumer education in the pharmacy consists of a pharmacy technician asking, "Do you have any questions?" and when the expected response of "no" is received, the consumer signs a document for no reason other than to acknowledge that a document needed to be signed. All they know is, if they get a generic, it costs less. Hurray for tiers.

In fact, tiers have worked so well that we are going to propose that you next apply them according to the *category* of drug, not just whether the drug happens to be preferred or generic within that category. And that's where the consumer education mentioned in the introduction comes in. Consider four categories:

1. **Lifestyle enhancing:** Medications used primarily to enhance one's ability to perform/achieve a lifestyle-related activity or goal. These are medications such as Viagra, Chantix, and Retin-A. All, or most of cost for these medications, would be assumed by the employee. These are essentially indulgences that happen to require prescriptions.

2. **Convenience:** Medications that produce outcomes not directly associated with the preservation of life or the normal functioning of body systems essential to life or medications with less costly treatment alternative(s) that generate similar clinical outcomes. Examples include Nexium, Clarinex, Provera, synthetic testosterone, and Penlac. These should have high copays.

3. **Life preserving:** Medications directly associated with the preservation of life or functioning of body systems essential to life. This is the largest of the groupings and includes medications for treatment of conditions such as infections, pain, seizures, depression, and cancer. Low copays would apply here.

4. **Business preserving:** Medications used to treat controllable chronic health conditions resulting in the highest levels of lost work time and long-term disability. This is typically the second largest grouping and includes medications for treatment of conditions such as hypertension, high cholesterol, diabetes, and asthma. These medications—especially the generic ones—should have invisibly low copays.

Look hard at these categories. If you think about it, the first—and even the second—categories really have no business being subsidized at all; they are merely consumer goods too hazardous to sell off a shelf. (This is what flexible spending accounts are for. Employees can pay for these indulgences themselves with pretax dollars.) If you do subsidize them, it's for recruitment/retention reasons. The third category contains drugs that people would typically have the good sense to obtain on their own, but you offer insurance so you cover them. But the fourth category, well, if you're an old-economy company and many of your employees are lifers, you want to make sure they control their chronic conditions, even if it means subsidizing more of the costs. (Hey, it beats paying them wellness incentives.)

So suppose you want to move in this direction, as some employers already are. It's rewarding, but there are a number of asterisks along the way. These asterisks are kind of nitpicky, if by "nitpicky" you mean "important to keep you out of jail," so we apologize for the level of detail. And remember this is a how-to book, so you can't complain if *Cracking Health Costs* tells you how to do something. You should have thought of that before you bought it.

First, even though prescription contraceptive methods might be considered as Category 2, they must now be covered at 100 percent under federal law. In addition, the inability to think clearly or reproduce were recently deemed disabilities, and, thus, care must now be taken to assure that coverage of adult attention deficit disorder treatments and fertility enhancers is equal to that of the majority of other medications.

Those are really the only two asterisks involving the law. The rest just involve various lessons others have learned so you don't have to. Consider those medications with multiple indications that cross over different categories. For example, Singulair is approved for the treatment of asthma (Category 4) as well as allergies (Category 2). Like the conditions other Category 4 drugs are designed to control, asthma can threaten life while seasonal allergies are more of a nuisance than a threat. The PBM can program its system to check for other prescription asthma treatments and when detected, automatically apply the lower member cost share for Singulair.

Occasionally a situation will require (gasp) prior authorization or (double-gasp) appeals to determine the appropriate cost share. For example, antifungals are used to treat systemic fungal infections that might come up once a decade in a large employer, as well as nail fungus. While systemic infections may threaten life, nail fungus is typically nothing more than an unsightly nuisance. These rare situations are probably easier to remedy than anticipate. This list of things to be remedied would probably include situations in which the low copay medication can't be tolerated or is contraindicated for some reason, but the appeals process already covers that stuff. Just make sure to resolve these appeals quickly.

Communication and Implementation

The next major lesson learned is the importance of communication. Remember, we're talking about employee education here, and your employees have a gazillion other things on their minds besides copays. You've done this type of communication before—when you communicated the multitier payment system itself. Now you need to do it again. It really does not matter how many times you produce lists of medications in the various categories. Employees are not going to pay attention to them. You can save a great deal of time and frustration by electronically posting the lists and focusing instead on clearly communicating the concepts.

A seasoned human resources manager knows that regardless of how many times a change is communicated, there will always be individuals who believe the change does not apply to them and therefore pay little attention. One way to deal with this phenomenon is to have the PBM send personalized letters to each consumer with a history of use of the targeted medications. The approximate cost difference may be best handled through use of an online pricing tool that adjusts for market cost changes as well as informs the consumer of alternative medications.

In the case of convenience medications, a last-minute benefits rush should be expected with budgeting to cover it.

The Close

Now it's time to close the deal with your employees. It should be no surprise that your employees have little understanding of the total costs of the prescription drug benefits they enjoy. Why then would we expect them to believe anything other than every prescription written should be covered in the same manner? They need to understand that just as the medical benefits for hospitalization do not cover items like plasma televisions and gourmet meals just because they're in a hospital, the prescription benefits should not cover lifestyle medications just because they require a prescription.

The more you communicate this, the more most will realize that, like most changes to benefits design, so far this change is a takeaway, because many more of your employees will have Category 1 and 2 medications than Category 4, the only category in which employee share goes down.

So why not make it a win-win? Measure the savings to your company from the increased copays themselves in Categories 1 and 2, and ballpark a guess for the long-term savings from improved compliance in Category 4. For example, uncontrolled hypertension will ultimately result in heart failure, kidney failure, stroke, and damage to the blood vessels supplying other vital organs and extremities. (Usually this happens after retirement. You'd need an actuary to weigh in on complication likelihood while employees are on your nickel.)

Once you've estimated the savings, there are a myriad of ways to share that wealth. I leave those to you. But all the communications in the world, while necessary, don't trump a visible financial benefit. Think of how you feel when you get a rebate check from a PBM. The difference would be this gainsharing check is real.

So there you have it. It's not so bad. There are some levers that can be pulled, including some special sauce you'll only read about here: negotiating spread with your PBM. During that negotiation, remember the lasting lesson from the Roman Empire: ultimately, Gaul won.

Chapter 5

Your Employees' Health Is Too Important to Be Left to the Doctors

S uppose you were an astronaut during the heyday of space explo-
ration, like John Glenn or Neil Armstrong or Larry Hagman. NASA
asks you if you want to fly to the moon. Would you respond: "No need.
I've seen the numbers and it's much cheaper and equally effective to
send a lunar probe and transmit the data back to us"?

Of course not. And therein lies one of the many reasons, perhaps
the most important, that specialists always seem to want to do diagnostics and procedures: they are specialists and this is what they do,
what they've trained to do, and—increasingly, as practices get purchased by hospitals—what their employer expects them to do.

Speaking of employers, now suppose that you are the NASA
supervisor who receives that response from an astronaut. Do you
reply: "Good point. That would be a great way to save money. I'll
put you in for a commendation"?

Again, of course not. You find an astronaut who *does* want to go to
the moon, because your ability to raise money from Congress depends
on meeting objectives. And your main objective is to put someone on
the moon, because if you don't, the Russians will—and then you'll lose
your job. Never mind that no one has ever quantified any long-term
economic benefit of putting a man on the moon. The important thing is
to be the country that does it first.

This clearly encapsulates one of the many reasons why hospitals and
freestanding clinics, particularly for-profit ones, encourage aggressive
physician interventions: because they are hospitals, they enjoy the
economic benefit of diagnostics and procedures not in the long term
but rather immediately, as soon as the claim gets approved for payment.
Just like the moon launches, providers get paid for completing the
procedure, whether or not it is necessary in an objective sense. And if
you have a review committee that tells the physician that the procedure is
not necessary, the physician will go somewhere else to do it.

There are many nuances in this dynamic involving many individuals and elements—physician, patient, and employer economics;
asymmetry of information and incomplete information; competitive
positioning; measuring outcomes; and government incentives. We'll
explore many of them in more detail throughout this chapter. But the
crucial thing to keep in mind is that all these nuances lead to one action
implication for you as a benefits manager. When it comes to high-cost
and profitable cases, never assume that a patient and a fee-for-service

doctor will arrive at the best course of treatment left to their own devices. And while I'll propose a solution in Chapter 7, Company-Sponsored Centers of Excellence, the goal for now is to get a grasp of the magnitude of the problem—the reasons that insured people in this country are overdiagnosed, overtreated, and generally overdoctored. (As we saw in Chapter 3, they are also overincentivized for prevention.)

Medicine Is Cheap, at Least at the Point of Service

Political writer PJ O'Rourke said it best: "If you think healthcare is expensive now, wait till you see how much it costs when it's free." The fact that someone else is picking up most of the check is indeed one reason we overconsume healthcare. It's not the only reason, but it enables the other reasons. Absence of an economic signal—a cost to offset perceived benefits—encourages consumption and competition to take place largely without regard to pricing.

My associate Al Lewis hates having blood drawn. He is probably not unique in that sense, but because he works in healthcare, he is closer to unique in knowing about the existence of something called a butterfly needle, which is machined to a much finer diameter than a regular needle. That attribute makes it somewhat less painful to the patient but also somewhat more expensive to whomever is paying. Al always asks the phlebotomist to substitute a butterfly needle for the regular one. Here are two possible answers that phlebotomist could give:

1. "That needle costs $5 more than the regular needle, so we'll have to charge you $5 more, and since it's not medically necessary but rather a patient convenience, we'll have to charge you that money out of pocket."
2. "Sure."

Which answer do you suppose the phlebotomist gives every time without hesitation? The answer provides a microcosm of healthcare economics: ask, and it's yours. This would never happen in, for example, a car dealership. If you want to add, for example, deluxe calfskin-lined power-assisted high-capacity cup holders, you'd get charged for them. This is true in most industries: when you want more, you pay more. But when you want more in healthcare, you don't pay more once you meet your annual deductible. Sometimes—as in the blood draw—you don't pay more, period.

Healthcare is not the only U.S. industry where wanting more and paying more are not matched one to one. Consider other underpriced and overconsumed items—fast food, housing, and gasoline. Each of those products enjoys explicit and/or hidden subsidies. In each case, consumers taking advantage of the subsidies to consume more than they otherwise would creates consequences. And they aren't just consequences for the taxpayers, who foot an enormous bill for individuals' overconsumption of government-subsidized offerings; they are also often consequences for the consumers themselves, who pay the price in obesity, underwater mortgages, and traffic.

Healthcare is like those industries, only worse, because "more" often costs next to nothing out-of-pocket. As obese as we Americans are now, imagine how much more we'd weigh if we could say "supersize me" every time we ate with no price consequences. Preposterous? That's essentially what happens in healthcare. Once we're in the system, we pay very little extra out of pocket to get much more care, creating the healthcare equivalent of rampant obesity.

As with obesity and food, ultimately we pay a hidden price for our overconsumption of healthcare, as we'll see next, as we list some of the causes, manifestations, and consequences of that overconsumption.

Too Much Healthcare Can Be Hazardous to Your Health

If there is one trend that epitomizes the overconsumption of healthcare, it's executive physicals. These in-depth half-day examinations, which often include extensive scanning, almost always reveal something, whether it's truly there or not. I'll let our colleague David McCann, editor of *CFO* magazine, tell a story. You want to listen to this guy, because if you don't take the steps outlined in this book to control health spending, your CFO will . . . and your own job description will be reduced to writing the rules for "Biggest Loser" competitions (which, by the way, are counterproductive—but that's a story for another book).

> *A good friend of mine underwent a "full-body screening" and a few suspicious cells were detected in his lung. So he had surgery, during which a hunk of one lung was removed. It was a difficult surgery, as you would imagine, and it took him a long time to recover. There was, of course, no cancer. Meanwhile, I had talked to my brother, who's a radiologist, who literally smacked himself in the forehead when he heard the story and said, "Every single person has suspicious*

cells. These full-body screenings and the surgeries they lead to are a shameful scam."

Far from being a rarity, findings like these—which often lead to surgeries like his—are so common that radiologists even have a disparaging name for them: "incidentalomas." Doctors can't ignore them—someone could sue if they truly turn out to be cancerous. Hence the finding itself creates the need for the surgery. Further, *Overdiagnosed* describes how the steady increase in imaging resolution is creating a parallel steady increase in these incidentalomas. For this and many other reasons, I strongly recommend against executive physicals, especially those involving scanning.

No sooner had I written this paragraph than the AHIP Smartbrief, which has never met a wellness intervention it didn't like, trumpeted exactly this situation. Via Christi Hospital's half-day screens for Intrust Bank leadership revealed an average of 1.1 new diagnoses per executive (on top of whatever diagnoses they already had, of course), most of which would need to be followed up with doctors and possibly diagnostics and treatments. The bank's spokesperson, in an understatement worthy of induction into the Wellness *Ignorati* Hall of Fame, observed: "It's still too early to see financial savings."

Via Christi's spokesperson was a bit blunter, admitting that these screens and follow-ups "offer another source of income" for the hospital.

The equivalent of the half-day executive physical for those of us in the "99 percent" is the biometric screen. Companywide screens are one of the many things that doctors are by and large opposed to (see the *Wall Street Journal*, February 20, 2013), the federal government eschews (the National Heart, Lung and Blood Institute recommends only once every five years for healthy working-age adults) but that the *ignorati* seemingly can't get enough of.

The good news about those screens is they will identify people at high risk for diabetes, one of the two diseases they most often target, and get them into a program well before they develop diabetes. The bad news (among other things) is that the evidence indicates that there is no difference in outcomes between people at high risk for diabetes who get screened and get early intervention and those who don't.

Renowned British medical journal *The Lancet* published a major study in November 2012 showing results of screenings followed by

10 years of follow-up on more than 20,000 people. This study was conducted according to tight academic specifications (requirements include having a hypothesis to be tested, statistically significant samples, a control, blinding, and so forth), as opposed to wellness industry specifications (requirements include owning a laptop). And because Britain has a national health system, follow-up was relatively straightforward. The results were unequivocal: there was zero health benefit to early screening in people to identify diabetics, if, like most diabetics, they received usual care for the next 10 years.[*]

This result justifies the U.S. Preventive Services Task Force's 2008 recommendation to restrict diabetes screening in the under-65 population to just those people with increased blood pressure. It also justifies the decision of many European countries to discontinue cardiometabolic screens (as described on www.medpage.com, April 19, 2013) due to 10-year follow-up studies showing them to be ineffective. What it does not justify is the wellness and consulting industries' insistence on doing more of them, more often, with higher penalties for non-compliance. Even so, it doesn't justify the section heading that too much healthcare is hazardous to your health (with full-body screens being a major exception), just that screening isn't necessarily helpful to your health. Read on.

Nebraska Wellness Program's "Hypocritic" Oath: First, Do Harm

As reported in *Business Management Daily* (January 3, 2013)—and of course the AHIP Smartbrief also conveyed its enthusiasm for this program, which is how I learned about it—the state of Nebraska's wellness program detected 500 cases of early-stage cancer among 6,200 participants, resulting in "early treatment." Unfortunately, *Overdiagnosed* (see the Bibliography) demonstrated quite convincingly that most of those so-called cancers found in screens fall into one of five categories:

(continued)

---

[*] It is also not clear that receiving anything more intensive than "usual care" will help enough to offset the higher costs of the more intensive intervention. It *may* be that this is the case, but the data is mixed. Even if it is the case, most complications would manifest themselves many years later, anyway.

(Continued)

1. False positive.
2. Clinically insignificant.
3. Nongrowing (or even shrinking, which, it turns out, happens quite a lot).
4. Nonlethal if it did grow.
5. The opposite—the cancer would kill the person whether detected now or later.

Six thousand two hundred commercially insured adults simply do not have more than a few important undiagnosed cancers for which early detection would be possible, correct, and beneficial, and there is no guarantee that this screen would even have caught those particular cancers. Here comes the "First, do harm" part: almost all of these 500 people were subjected to debilitating, distressing, hazardous, futile, and expensive "early treatment" due to this state's consultants and vendors failing to read the current literature, which would have indicated that most of these people shouldn't even have been tested. And, by the way, the state also lied about its savings figures. Those 500 people following up on alleged cancers would have overwhelmed even the fictitious savings generally claimed from these programs.

I know you're thinking: "This program must be an outlier." And indeed it is . . . in the other direction: in 2012, it won the C. Everett Koop Award for Wellness Program Excellence.

Along with diabetes, the other major focus of these biometric screens is heart disease. Heart disease is no doubt a killer, and there are sobering statistics somewhere about the number of people experiencing preventable heart attacks every year. Fortunately, "sobering" is not a synonym for "correct," and if a statistic about preventable heart disease strikes you as sobering, it is probably because it's wrong.

Here is the rather nonsobering *actual* statistic: the annual rate of heart attacks in the commercially insured working-age population is only about 1 in 500. Next, let's add some educated guesswork. Feel free to substitute your own guesses—they won't change the overall answer:

◆ If you omit the people with known risk factors or preexisting heart disease—people who don't need the screening because they already know they are at risk—that number falls to about 1 in 2,000.

◆ If you then count only the people who could have their heart disease detected via a rudimentary screen, thereby eliminating those whose subsequent heart attacks are not readily predictable, that number falls further, possibly to about 1 in 4,000. This ratio in reality is probably even more unfavorable, as cholesterol, particularly the "bad" cholesterol, turns out to be a very primitive marker for heart disease, both overinclusive (leading to much more treatment) and underpredictive (many people with acceptable "bad" cholesterol nonetheless have heart attacks).*

So a $40 biometric screen will find at best one avoidable heart attack in every 4,000 people . . . at a cost of $160,000. Add in, for instance, $200 in incentives and $20 in time off from work to persuade people to participate, and you've now created the *million-dollar heart attack screen*.

And keep in mind that *find* is not the same as *avoid*. I don't think anyone has statistics on what proportion of potential heart attacks are avoided. If we generously assume that fully half of avoidable heart attacks can indeed be avoided, the cost per avoidable heart attack that actually is avoided becomes $2 million.

You might say at this point: "Well, maybe I can't justify spending $2 million in purely economic terms to prevent an employee from having a heart attack (which typically costs five figures to treat and recover from, including follow-up and lost work time). But a heart attack entails a human cost of pain, suffering, and possibly even risk of death, as well. And I would happily spend 2 million bucks to avoid that cost."

A well-intentioned thought, to be sure. But the trouble is that you don't know *which one* of the people being screened as being high-risk is going to be that 1 in 4,000. And that's where the "too much healthcare

* Seth S. Martin, Michael J. Blaha, Mohamed B. Elshazly, Eliot A. Brinton, Peter P. Toth, John W. McEvoy, Parag H. Joshi, et al., "Friedewald Estimated versus Directly Measured Low-Density Lipoprotein Cholesterol and Treatment Implications," *Journal of the American College of Cardiology*, available online March 21, 2013, ISSN 0735-1097, 10.1016/j.jacc.2013.01.079, www.sciencedirect.com/science/article/pii/S073510971301098X.

can be hazardous to your health" part comes in. Two to three percent of the people screened—about 1 in 40—will be instructed to follow up with their doctors. Follow the arithmetic here: 1 in 40 means that 100 people will get referred. However, only one of the people receiving this advice would actually have a heart attack if he or she failed to do so (and may even have one anyway, despite that follow-up care). But those other 99 will get extra doctor visits, prescriptions, and possibly cardiologist referrals. And cardiologists almost always order further testing, since their professional risk of doing nothing is quite high.

What is the result of "almost always ordering further testing"? According to *Overtreated* author Shannon Brownlee, invasive cardiac testing and procedures are performed almost 2 million times a year. To put this in perspective, the number of babies born in the United States is only about twice that. So at current rates of testing and procedures, half of all people will eventually have an average of one invasive test or procedure. Are our hearts so fragile or ill-evolved that such a massive proportion of our population needs (at a minimum) dye injected into them to make sure they are pumping correctly? Take a look at your own company's heart attack rates—that 1 in 500 figure won't be far off—and then decide if reducing that overall 1-in-500 annual chance to perhaps 1-in-1,000 is worth sending half your employees for invasive testing at some point. (Admittedly, that statistic is a little misleading because many of those employees wouldn't get the invasive test until after they retire.)

And here are your chances of success: once the substantial countrywide decline in heart events is taken into account, no company or health plan ever measured covering more than 100,000 people—about the level at which you can be sure of a result—has ever reduced that rate by half once the secular decline in heart attacks is taken into account, even over 10 years.

You might be thinking, "Especially considering the small chance of success, that sounds like a lot of inappropriateness." But I haven't even gotten to the inappropriate part yet. With the exceptions of cardiac procedures actually being done in the throes of a heart attack (U.S. medicine at its best: timely, responsive, and effective) and a few other clearly delineated cohorts, there is no clear evidence that these procedures actually help people to avoid heart attacks, as *Overtreated* shows at length. Among other pieces of evidence, there is no correlation between the rate of cardiac testing and procedures in a given geography and the rate of heart attacks.

Many primary care doctors know this. Paul Levy, who formerly ran Beth Israel Deaconess Hospital in Boston, recalls the time he needed a stress test as a requirement for participating in an ocean kayaking trip in Patagonia. His PCP refused to order it. She said: "Because he knows who you are, the cardiologist will be especially attuned to any odd peculiarity about your heartbeat. He will then feel the need, because you are president of the hospital, to do a diagnostic catheterization. Then, there will be some kind of complication and you will end up being harmed. But the reality is that whatever peculiarity he finds has probably existed for decades. There is no history of heart disease in your family. You cycle 100 miles per week and play soccer for hours every week, and you have never had a symptom that would indicate a circulatory problem. Therefore, I will not authorize a stress test."

Also, the literature is quite clear that stenting people without unstable angina has no better outcomes than the diet-and-exercise solution. But because a stent is "doing something" and (see first section) basically free, many if not most people will follow the doctor's recommendation and have stents inserted.

Still, the doctor is the professional, and he has all the data in front of him and is working on your employees' behalf. So he wouldn't recommend an invasive procedure unless it was truly indicated . . . or would he? As the next section explains, he just might.

LIKE CORPORATIONS, DOCTORS ARE PEOPLE, TOO

There is an inherent conflict of interest in any fee-for-service transaction. The hairstylist, stockbroker, real estate agent, and butcher all make more if they can sell you more. For instance, some Jiffy Lubes show you your air filter and then ask you if you want it replaced. Most people accept their offer because those things can look dirty to a layperson after only a couple of thousand miles, even if they are designed to last much longer. A little slippery on their part, perhaps, but at least you have to weigh the cost before agreeing to pay it, and you get to see the filter. The transaction is literally and figuratively transparent, but there is still what economists call an "asymmetry of information." The mechanic knows how dirty an air filter needs to be before replacement, and you don't.

In healthcare, your employee usually doesn't have to weigh the cost because a huge, faceless corporation is paying for most of it. The doctor can advise whatever he wants, and most people go along with the recommendation—and it's not a dirty air filter they're worrying about. It's their life.

Don't take my word for it, though; the following chart shows the comparative rates per 100,000 people of heart surgeries and angioplasties for the United States and countries with equivalent or longer life expectancies.

Canada	229
France	196
Italy	157
New Zealand	187
Switzerland	118
United Kingdom	169
United States	579

This data is from the 2007 Organisation for Economic Co-operation and Development (OECD) "Health at a Glance" (page 75). Though the most recent reports don't collect the data the same way, they show similar results: the U.S. rate is twice the OECD average . . . and yet Americans have a lower-than-average life expectancy.

The following are some reasons for this overtreatment that I've collected over the years, mostly from doctors themselves, particularly for cancer and surgery. You'll notice the same Jiffy Lube-type asymmetry of information here, as well.

Reason #1 is the most obvious: like most people, most doctors get paid more for doing more. (This is even true when the organization they work for does not.) I'll provide examples of how to mitigate or eliminate this factor in the chapter on Company-Sponsored Centers of Excellence. And bear in mind I am not the only one to figure this out. The Accountable Care Organization (ACO) movement is a response to this conflict of interest, as was the development of capitated practices before that and HMOs even before that. (I'll address ACOs in the next chapter.)

Don't Take My Word for It, Part Two: Here's What a Cardiothoracic Surgeon Has to Say

The following is written by Dr. Mary Bourland, cardiovascular and thoracic surgeon and director of clinical integration for Mercy Health Systems. Dr. Bourland has screened over 10,000 women for heart and vascular disease and educated twice as many. She was the recipient of the Women of Distinction Award, her program listed in the Top 100 Heart Hospitals, and Money *listed her vascular program among the top 25 in the nation.*

After performing thousands of heart surgeries over my lifetime and following my patients for years on end, I know that the notion of having specialists as the sole gatekeepers to surgery is deeply ineffective.

Rita (fictional name) is a 55-year-old, diabetic, hypertensive, moderately overweight, white female. She is a single mom, has four children and works 40 hours a week at a local grocery. Parts of her job involve lifting and stooping at strange angles. Rita has been starting to have chest pain with exertion. It goes away with resting for 5 to 10 minutes. Rita's primary care doctor performs a stress test showing she needs a heart catheterization ("cath"). Dr. John (fictional name), a cardiologist, performs the cath that demonstrates diffuse multivessel disease with two arteries that have 70 to 80 percent blockages.

What are Rita's actual medical options, in theory?

A. Have Dr. John place two drug-eluding stents.
B. Undergo bypass surgery.
C. Practice medical management.

Any of the above could be the right answer. It depends.

But what choice is Rita given, in practice? Probably none of the above. If Dr. John feels it's appropriate, he goes ahead and places the stents *during the cardiac catheterization itself,* thus becoming the gatekeeper of the patient's artery disease. (By the way, he is well-rewarded financially to choose the stent-now approach, which takes little extra time at that point.)

(continued)

(Continued)

But herein lies the problem: Dr. John has just usurped the role of gatekeeper from Rita's primary care physician—despite the fact that the PCP knows Rita the best, and knowing a patient can be critical.* Most times, there is no hurry or medical necessity to proceed with stenting at the time of the cath; it's only necessary in the case of a heart attack or unstable symptoms. So why not allow the patient to discuss the risks and alternatives of *all* available treatments? Will Rita be able to afford and be compliant with the expensive medications that she will have to take to keep her new stents from clotting off? If she is sent for bypass surgery, will she lose her job because her sternum hurts each time she lifts anything? Social influences, as eloquently outlined in the past by Nortin Hadler, MD, and Otis Brawley, MD, (see, for instance, *How We Do Harm*, in the bibliography) have as much impact on health and recovery as any part of medicine.

There are two major differences between this and the Jiffy Lube asymmetry: the patient doesn't get to see his old arteries before agreeing to ream them out with a stent, and the stent is "free." Very few patients lying on the table, paying with someone else's money, are going to decline a cardiologist saying: "You need a stent." If you don't dispute the Jiffy Lube mechanic, you're not going to dispute the cardiologist.

Conflicts can even exist where doctors are salaried in some academic centers. Many doctors can get more research money if they can generate more income in the department—and more income requires more procedures.

Reason #2 is that doctors often don't keep up with advances in medicine. For instance, ulcer treatment was perhaps the last great

---

* Knowing the patient is key and often undervalued. *Downton Abbey* fans will recall (WARNING: SPOILER ALERT for people who are hopelessly behind on their DVRed primetime period dramas) that the reason Sybil died was that the high-priced specialist swooping in from London thought she just had thick ankles whereas the local general practitioner who had known her all her life knew she didn't and that those were swollen ankles indicating eclampsia.

example in which a pill could almost unequivocally produce outcomes better than an operation could, and instantly obsoleted ulcer surgeries. Yet doctors still performed 40,000 elective peptic ulcer surgeries *three years* after the drug Tagamet was introduced.

Reason #3: The patient wants the surgery, and the doctor figures that the patient will simply get it from someone else if he declines to perform it. And because many doctors are judged on patient satisfaction, saying no means dissatisfying a patient and possibly causing a ding on the doctor's own performance review or bonus. A corollary is that doctors feel that patients should have the right to choose a surgery once they've explained the pros and cons—even if the surgeon or primary care physician says that the minuses outweigh the pluses. By definition, patients should not be permitted to opt for surgery where the negatives exceed positives—or at a minimum, such surgeries should not be underwritten by the payer-employer.

Reason #4 is that the surgeon believes his professional judgment and experience trumps science. The typical language used to justify the procedure is: "My (or many) patients report good results." That is neither science nor evidence.

Reason #5 cites the Balkanization of healthcare: a doctor looks at a patient and sees a blocked artery. He or she wants to fix that artery, often with little regard for the fact that the patient may be too feeble for the surgery or that a nonsurgical medical alternative might be equally effective and even safer for the patient. Dr. Bourland (introduced in the boxed feature) also notes that some cardiac surgeons will accept fairly advanced diabetics for bypass surgeries, even though their blood vessels may be too fragile to be stitched safely.

A brilliant acquaintance of mine named Dan Ariely has written a great book called *The (Honest) Truth About Dishonesty: How We Lie to Everyone—Especially Ourselves*. That book offers a complete picture about how otherwise good people can turn dishonest. And while Dan's book is not solely about doctors, it describes how a culture of dishonesty can corrupt even well-intentioned people. It's easy to infer from that assumption that a culture of procedures can pressure a physician not doing enough procedures into doing more.

Reason #6: Like people in many professions, doctors often have employers. They're frequently large group practices or hospitals that are trying to gain share in a marketplace, which they achieve by doing as many procedures as possible. This is the syndrome that ACOs are supposed to cure—and when you read the chapter on ACOs, you can decide if you think they will.

Reason #7: The official government-established rules are distorted to enhance the income of "proceduralists" (specialists doing procedures). This is not my imagination or hyperbole. The rules were detailed in *Health Affairs* (March 12, 2012), a widely read and highly authoritative journal. These rules, which apply specifically to Medicare payments yet generally set the tone for non-Medicare payments, are established, not surprisingly, by a committee that is overwhelmingly composed of proceduralists. This group is called the Relative Value Scale Update Committee (RUC), and since its inception in the 1980s, the percentage gap between primary care and proceduralist income has more than doubled. (You can visit www.ReplacetheRUC.net to gain a more in-depth understanding.)

To put a few numbers on the proceduralist bias in the United States generally, compare what surgeons receive for hip replacements in the United States versus other countries, according to *Health Affairs* (September 2011):

Australia	$1,943
Canada	$652
France	$1,340
Germany	$1,251
United Kingdom	$2,160
United States (privately insured)	$3,996

Reason #8: Caution. This notion that a doctor can get into more malpractice hot water by doing less than by doing more has been analyzed by others so we won't repeat, except to add an anecdote. One colleague, Gary Glissman, writes: "Our situation involved an unnecessary hysterectomy that was suggested by an excellent OB-GYN physician who was just trying to be very cautious. Fortunately, we had access to one of the best gynecological cancer experts in the U.S., who informed us that an aggressive approach was likely not needed and there were other options. That was two years ago and the opinion was right on target. As a result, our family member avoided a routine but still risky surgery, not to mention all of the cost and life adjustments that would have come along with the procedure."

What makes this story bookworthy is not that it shows the system working, but rather that it shows the system *not* working. Gary, as his (tremendous) luck would have it, is the chief operating officer of a urology cancer center. He's therefore closely aligned with the first-ever cancer second-opinion network, www.canceropinions.com, which is how he was able to access the renowned expert. The emergence of companies like CancerOpinions validates one theme of this chapter and Chapter 7: access to second opinions by nationally known sub-specialists—who themselves do not have to rely on the treating physician for second opinions on their own cases—is an excellent way to avoid unnecessary surgeries.

Unfortunately, 99.9 percent of the population would have followed the original doctor's recommendation and undergone the hysterectomy . . . and those 99.9 percent work for you, not Gary. Hence, as long as malpractice laws remain the same, the burden of avoiding the "doing more" caution trap will fall on you.

Hospitals Want Volume

The *New York Times* (November 30, 2012) reported on a "hospital war" taking place in Boise, Idaho. Hospitals started buying physician practices several years ago, and now the two largest ones employ roughly half the physicians for many miles around. The article states: "Many of the independent doctors complain that both hospitals . . . have too much power over every aspect of the medical pipeline, dictating which tests and procedures to perform, how much to charge and which patients to admit."

By itself that statement is journalistic hearsay. However, it makes sense when we consider it in the context of the economics of two hospitals bidding against each other to buy a physician practice. The ensuing bidding war ends with a price justifiable only if volume (and fees) can *increase* after the purchase, to cover the cost of money committed to the purchase as well as the physician incomes. It would make no economic sense for a hospital to pay top dollar for a stream of revenue and then try to undercut that stream.

The article goes on to say: "Across the country, doctors who sold their practices and signed on as employees have similar criticisms. They describe in lawsuits and interviews growing pressure to meet their new employers' financial goals—often by performing unnecessary tests and procedures or by admitting patients who do not need a hospital stay."

Volume creates a self-reinforcing cycle for reasons other than revenue, too. For instance, death rates from bypass operations correlate with the number of bypass operations performed. Two hundred procedures a year seems to be the inflection point. The healthcare *cognoscenti* would never schedule their own bypass at a hospital with less volume than that, yet half the hospitals in the country licensed for cardiac surgery do fewer than 200 procedures. (The good news is that the large majority of procedures are performed in hospitals in which more than 200 are performed annually.) Hospitals get publicly graded on their cardiac surgery death rates, and outliers would be noted in the local media. Likewise, as with any other good, the cost of each unit declines as volume increases.

On the flip side, it wouldn't even be possible to grade hospitals (and hence their surgeons) based on procedures *not* done without either grossing the number of procedures up to the level of the county—as *The Dartmouth Atlas* has done—or through very careful record review and due diligence, as the Company-Sponsored Centers of Excellence chapter recommends for tertiary care (and as the Mercy Spine Center sidebar demonstrates).

DOCTORS OWN ANCILLARY FACILITIES

There are ironclad rules against referring someone to a diagnostic facility in exchange for a fee. However, the rules about making even more money off one's own in-house diagnostic facilities are much murkier, for the simple reason that it is difficult to separate the advantages of patient convenience and physician control from the rather obvious financial advantages to the physician at your expense. It therefore comes as no surprise that physician groups that own diagnostic equipment order more tests versus those that need to refer out.

Summary

This chapter has catalogued a massive array of forces aligned to maximize your employees' use of high-cost diagnostics and procedures: point-of-service economics, the supply-creates-demand effect of screening, information asymmetry, physician incentives/culture, hospital demands, and ownership of diagnostic equipment. It's all a bit disheartening—perhaps to the point that it would seem like not much can be done.

The good news, however, is that we always end each section with an easy-to-implement action step. And nothing could be easier than the action step for this section: read Part II. Chapter 7 covers how to opt out of this cycle by using national or regional Company-Sponsored Centers of Excellence. This is followed by a chapter on how to make the best of your current provider configuration by favoring the higher quality local hospitals for more routine procedures and medical events.

Chapter **6**

Are New Delivery Models Déjà Vu All Over Again, Again?

Management is fad-driven. Don't believe me? Think of all the management fads that have come and gone over the years: management by objective, managing your strategic portfolio, reengineering, right-sizing, intrapreneurship, outsourcing, insourcing, rightsourcing. . . . Basically anything that follows the cliché, "We're facing a new paradigm" is a fad. No doubt most contain a grain of truth, but none are a substitute for exercising good judgment.

Managing health benefits is likewise fad-driven. The difference between general management fads and health benefit management fads is that the latter tend to die a slower death. This is because health benefit math is murky enough that consultants, vendors, and health systems can convince you that their fads are working for many years after those fallacies should have become perfectly apparent.

Accountable Care Organizations (ACO) and Patient-Centered Medical Homes (PCMH) may be two such fallacies. And while both the rationales and (in the case of PCMH) outcomes should give major pause, they are sweeping the country, nonetheless. Our advice to benefits administrators: take a deep breath, let others go first, and don't automatically believe published results, since the most publicized PCMH result has been thoroughly discredited, so much so that the alleged savings from PCMH in general seem to be generating a second, more critical reevaluation already, compelling proponents to redirect their enthusiasm toward the less easily discredited but also less compelling notion of intangible benefits from the enhanced access they offer.

There is a reason for our bifurcated viewpoint. ACOs and PCMHs couldn't be more different, yet the two are often deployed together when a PCMH is part of an ACO and often discussed in the same sentence (such as this one). However, ACOs are aimed squarely at controlling excess, while the PCMH model addresses the increasingly quaint and discredited belief that (commercially insured) Americans in populated areas lack sufficient access to primary care.

This chapter addresses both in turn, and—consistent with our how-to focus—concludes by providing the steps you must take to determine whether either model is saving you money. That sentence of course assumes you've ignored, perhaps under duress, our advice two paragraphs back to let others pioneer these innovations.

Accountable Care Organizations

These are groupings of hitherto generally independent doctors, hospitals, and other providers who—at considerable expense and adhering to considerable regulations—have banded together into coordinated entities. As such, their success in controlling costs and increasing quality may qualify them for a contractual bonus. The idea is that groups financially responsible for the care of a population will be more judicious in their deployment of it. (If this sounds familiar, the reason we chose this chapter title is that this was also the idea behind HMOs and, more recently, behind fully capitated physician practices.)

Déjà Vu All Over Again, Again, Again

Meet the New Model—Same as the Old Models (DM and Wellness)

When Al attended an ACO/PCMH conference in early 2013, he expected to hear presentations informing hospitals about the importance of improving safety, reducing overtreatment, changing incentives for proceduralists, and so on. Instead he heard presentations on how to engage patients and get them to change behaviors. There was not one word in one presentation about the changes that need to take place *within* the four walls. Apparently, it's all the patients' fault; we aren't engaged and therefore we don't comply. (Revisit this sidebar after you read Al's personal story of noncompliance two pages hence.)

If there is one thing that the healthcare industry should have learned from previous efforts—first by health plans (disease management), and then by employers attempting essentially the same thing (wellness)—it's that engaging people and convincing them to change behavior is hard. Doctors *should* succeed in many cases where outsiders or employers failed, due to their trust relationship with the patient. However, increasing engagement using the physician practice channel also costs far more than making a few phone calls does. An organization needs a far higher engagement rate just to break even on the far higher expense. It's also not a lock that they will achieve that engagement rate, not to mention behavior change. Exhibit A: smokers already have doctors who tell them to quit.

Finally, Al also learned that none of these ACO/PCMH Einsteins can measure savings, either—and it isn't that hard. They should just count up the events, procedures, and errors they are trying to reduce year over year, and see if that total declines. And yet they prefer to befuddle themselves—and you and me—with claims of savings on people with multiple chronic conditions and complex cases. But these two categories will decline in cost as a group, even if you do nothing, after they endure the high-cost events that qualified them for the program in the first place. Then, other, previously unremarkable people become high utilizers, creating no net change in costs.

I must distinguish this model from the Company-Sponsored Centers of Excellence (CSCOEs) model (see Chapter 7) that I *do* embrace, because of one specific major difference. CSCOEs generally grew up as ACOs. Most physicians are salaried to a large degree if not totally, which means that they only have minimal (if any) incentive to overdiagnose, overtreat, and especially overoperate. Excess care is simply not part of the CSCOE culture.

Other chapters in this book discount the notion that employers can bribe or otherwise voluntarily persuade people to act in their own best interest, that is, as their employer would define the employee's own best interest and possibly as an objective person would define it. That's a tough enough task, but ACOs don't stop there. They layer on certain incentives to control utilization in fee-for-service delivery systems whose culture and compensation has historically been—and still largely is—driven by volume. We've seen how hard it is to persuade people to act in their own best interest, but any continuation of volume-driven payment means that ACOs must try to persuade some specialists to act *against* their own short-term financial interest, because many if not most specialists in an ACO still earn the large majority of their income from activity. Even if the economics of activity are not as completely compelling as they otherwise would have been, surgeons, in particular, prefer activity to counseling, because surgery keeps surgeons sharp, and it is, after all, what they do, as their name implies. They didn't spend 10 years in post-college training to become counselors.

There may be a group incentive to control expense; however, it is typically in the 5 percent range and usually allocated across many people based on overall performance. Unlike the naturally occurring ACOs that we recommend as CSCOEs, the health systems upon which this ACO label is overlaid had to be persuaded to voluntarily become an ACO. They then had to persuade doctors to join. Since voluntary persuasion rarely involves takeaways, these provider groupings were formed using offers, not threats.* Medicare, for instance, allows ACOs to choose between payment models with a small bonus potential and payment models with larger bonus potential but some penalty potential. See if you can guess which option most ACOs are selecting.

Also, much of what drives a hospital's perceived quality and reputation is volume; hospitals are often paid per stay rather than per day. Volume tends to reduce cost per stay, meaning that increasing volume raises not just revenues but profit margins, as well. What a hospital considers a positive outcome, and what you as an employer consider a positive outcome are two different animals. High utilization is a positive outcome for hospitals, where it is a cost for you.

Another caveat: it costs many millions of dollars to become an ACO. This cost needs to be captured in any fee they charge you.

Nonetheless, it is indeed possible that some of these new ACOs could reduce costs by driving better outcomes. So we can't say that ACOs won't eventually save money, that ACOs are automatically a bad idea (they aren't), and that you should avoid ACOs at all costs. Your best approach is simply to let others go first. However, we can't say the same about PCMHs, which are covered in the next section.

---

* One exception is Massachusetts, which has moved far out in front of the rest of the country by favoring global provider reimbursement for some patient groups. This approach doesn't necessarily solve the problem of paying individual specialists for activity. However, it does multiply the overall group incentive to control costs and is a "threat" in that downside is possible for providers as a group. It also moves the issue of adverse selection to the doctors, some of whom won't take on new patients with health problems. It is too early to tell if this approach is succeeding.

Why ACO Pay-for-Performance Models Aren't a No-Brainer

See the *Health Affairs* blog post by behavioral economists Steffie Woolhandler and Dan Ariely entitled, "Will Pay-for-Performance Backfire?" (October 11, 2012), http://healthaffairs.org/blog/2012/10/11/will-pay-for-performance-backfire-insights-from-behavioral-economics/. It summarizes past research into whether financial incentives to change physician behavior or, more important, outcomes, were successful . . . and comes up empty. They also examine pay-for-performance schemes outside of healthcare, such as teacher bonuses, blood donation, picking up children after day care, and puzzle-solving. They conclude that changing financial incentives may be very overrated, and that culture, passion, and mission play a bigger role than expected in decision-making. (Hence, our emphasis on specific medical centers that feature all three.)

These two may be right, but—more important for your purposes—they are not obviously wrong, like most other studies referenced in this book. (Al makes his living partly by proving healthcare studies and outcomes wrong, but this blog posting easily passes his validity sniff test.) This is why our recommendation is to let others lead the way. If they are right, you've avoided a costly detour. Odds are, even if Woolhandler and Ariely are wrong, there will be plenty of stumbles along the way that you can let others make before the ultimate delivery model crystallizes.

Patient-Centered Medical Homes

PCMHs are nowhere near as complex as ACOs. They mainly focus on primary care and case management, to more closely monitor chronically ill people and provide earlier diagnosis and treatment in general. They pay primary physicians more, and physicians commit to doing more in exchange. They operate according to the notion that greater access to care will reduce costs down the road. However, as we've already shown with wellness, biometric screens, and disease management, throwing more care at people may *add* cost . . . and actually create more problems than it solves.

The good news is that patient-centered medical homes are a terrific boon for the worried well. As Al wrote in *Why Nobody Believes the Numbers*—before tearing apart mathematically impossible medical home savings claims in detail— "I'm not an anti-homite. I'm in a PCMH and I love it." He goes on to describe extended hours, physicians' prompt availability, and easily obtained referrals. His practice essentially provides concierge medicine without the concierge fee, at the expense of the insurer or self-insured employer.

Al has more recently added a new anecdote. After the first taping of his new radio show (*The Big Fix* in case anyone wants to check www.wamu.org to see if it's still on the air), his producer asked if he had a cold, which he didn't. Not wanting to be fired his first day on the job, and recalling that he had a deviated septum, he immediately called his PCP for advice.

This being a highly responsive PCMH (as most are), his PCP almost as immediately set up an appointment for him to see an ear, nose, and throat (ENT) specialist, who determined that his stuffiness was likely being caused not by the septum but by polyps. The ENT suggested surgery (cautioning that the polyps could grow back afterward), steroid nasal spray, or the spray combined with a three-week course of antibiotics. "So," she asked after quite literally six minutes explaining the options, "which do you want to do?"

"Um, shouldn't we do the most conservative therapy first?" he inquired.

"Well, you could," she replied, using a tone of voice that, to Al at least, implied that only an imbecile actually would.

This perfectly summarizes the problem with the PCMH model. Al's access to physician care was so unfettered that within five business days of his first call to the PCP, he was about to be scheduled for a completely unnecessary surgery.

There are fully six postscripts to this anecdote. First, the surgeon didn't mention any drawbacks or risks of taking a course of antibiotics for three full weeks. However, most of us know that antibiotics are far from harmless, which is why they still require prescriptions, almost a century after the discovery of penicillin. Second, the surgeon didn't even hypothesize that the cause was bacterial. She asserted instead that "some people report getting relief by using the antibiotics," which, more than coincidentally, is also the classic "before" comment in an evidence-based medicine continuing education session.

Third, she also scheduled a CT scan for Al's sinuses to take place three days after the appointment. This short amount of time would not have given the nasal spray a chance to work. And Al already had a diagnosis, so there was nothing she could learn from the scan other than whether the spray was working (which didn't require a scan, just a scope). Although the appointment was conveniently made for him, he had enough sense to cancel it. Al (unlike many other people) was fortunate enough to know that—among other excellent reasons for avoiding them—sinus scans introduce a disproportionate amount of radiation into one's skull, as well as a disproportionate amount of dye into one's veins.

A Clip-and-Save List of Questions Your Employees Should Be Trained to Ask Their Doctors Before Agreeing to Any Nonroutine Test

(Courtesy of our resident overtreatment expert, Brian Klepper, and the American College of Physicians)

> Do you have the results of my previous test? (if indeed, you have had one).
>
> Will the test results change anything? What do you hope to learn from them?
>
> What is the probability and potential consequence of a false-positive result?
>
> Is there a potential danger if you don't order this test?
>
> Does the test itself post any potential dangers or complications?

Fourth, a close reading of the medication package insert revealed that one of the nasal spray's potential side effects was hoarseness—precisely the condition that Al was trying to alleviate.

Fifth, Al solved his immediate problem by simply talking louder and letting the studio engineer calibrate his volume instead. If, by the time you read this, *The Big Fix* ("Policy without Politics") is no longer being aired, it won't be because Al's voice sounds like that guy on *Boardwalk Empire* whose vocal chords were blown up in World War I. It will be because, in Al's own low-talker words, "I'm not a very good radio host."

Indeed, a few people did complain, not without justification, about other aspects of his hosting skills, but no one wrote in to say: "This guy sounds like he needs his polyps removed."

So, Al canceled his sinus scan, stopped taking his medication, and never scheduled a follow-up visit. And that brings us to the sixth and final postscript: Al received a bad "report card" from Medimpact, his health plan's PBM, giving him only one star out of a possible four due to his failure to renew his nasal spray, a failure that they said "may need immediate attention."

In short, fortunately for Al and his insurance company (and his employer, if he had one), he became one of those noncompliant patients that ACOs and PCMHs complain about.

This anecdote is a microcosm of the many reasons that the PCMH is not only unlikely to live up to its promise to reduce costs, but actually may increase them. The idea that a PCMH saves money (or provides better care without increasing costs, which seems to be its proponents' evolving position) is built on at least six explicit and implicit assumptions:

1. Access generates more preventive care.
2. Early detection is a good thing, and PCMHs offer more of it.
3. The PCP and case manager can coordinate care to keep people from falling through the cracks.
4. Conversely, more PCP supervision of care, combined with an electronic medical record, will prevent redundant or unnecessary resource use for those who don't need it.
5. The PCP knows what he or she is doing.
6. PCP intervention can help control your overall costs.

Let's examine each of these in turn.

1. Access generates more preventive care.

This five-word statement is at least 80 percent true. Access generates more care. Perhaps some of it is preventive. We'll get to that later. However, I've found while managing very large private benefit plans that people either are fine with going to the doctor or they aren't. Doctors are already fairly available; making them more so won't convince people who don't want to go to the doctor to suddenly get religion. And the worried well will end up visiting physicians for complaints that would self-resolve.

In-pharmacy clinics are an excellent example of this—a segment that virtually didn't exist 12 years ago, but is now the fastest-growing in primary care. Despite the growth of this segment, try to find an office-based physician who says: "My practice isn't remotely as busy as it was now that CVS has a clinic down the street." Most in-store clinics cater to immediate needs; they usually don't even require appointments. They aren't set up for lengthy relationship-building visits, and, in any case, most health providers view their jobs at these clinics as stopping points, not careers— building relationships with patients who already have primary care doctors is not a priority for most of them.

So access doesn't automatically equate to prevention. Consider Al's polyps; despite the Internet speed with which he received specialist care and an appointment for an unnecessary CT scan, he observes that patients must schedule preventive physicals at his practice at least three months in advance.

Further, one must question the notion that states: if some prevention is good, then more is better. Look up a blog called "Common Sense Family Doctor." The December 22, 2012, post (http://commonsensemd.blogspot.com/2012/12/false-alarms-and-unrealistic.html) provides links to many articles that question this conventional wisdom, like the massive study described in the January 15, 2013, issue of *JAMA Internal Medicine*, which reported that more preventive visits did not increase longevity, only diagnoses. And America does not suffer from a shortage of diagnoses.

2. **Early detection is a good thing and there is more of it in PCMHs.**

Like prevention, detection generates more care, period. And also like prevention, detection is not an unmitigated boon. As noted in the last chapter's discussion of screenings, even "accurate" tests mathematically lead to large numbers of false positives—which then generate follow-up testing, which is expensive, inconvenient, and keeps your employees away from work. And as with biometric screens, much of what PCP visits detect would never become clinically significant, anyway. *Overdiagnosed* puts prehypertension, prediabetes, hyperlipidemia, and osteoporosis in that category. In each case, the threshold lab value for what constitutes disease was lowered by a committee largely composed of drug industry representatives, and in each case no one has yet proven that treatment provides value exceeding the possible side effects at those newly lowered thresholds.

Remarkably, early detection may finally be on the decline. The consensus, for at least some disease categories, is that detection creates more costs than benefits. Guidelines for mammograms and colonoscopies have been relaxed, and the notoriously unreliable PSA test for prostate cancer has finally fallen into disrepute (except in the wellness industry and Nebraska).

Like everything, detection reaches a point of diminishing return. Why invest in a system designed to encourage more detection if we've reached that point? Yes, we heard you say it a few pages ago—you have an employee whose condition wasn't detected in a timely fashion and who is now very ill. But statistically speaking, you are much more likely to have employees who were caused harm by overdetecting, and that's why these detection guidelines have been relaxed.

3. **The PCP and case manager prevent people with multiple conditions from falling through the cracks.**

This is probably true—and is indeed probably the best argument for moving to a PCMH model. It's also one of the three reasons why the PCMH undertaken for Medicare HMO members by Pennsylvania's Geisinger Health System has demonstrated good outcomes. The other two are that Geisinger is a "naturally occurring" ACO with mostly salaried physician staff, and the PCMH enrolled only patients 65 and older.

Your employees are by definition commercially insured. But ask yourself how many of those employees are so fragile that they need you to follow them this closely while also considering that being closely followed isn't guaranteed to prevent adverse events. To estimate a number of people who will benefit from a care manager's watchful eye, consider the following ballpark figures. About 6 percent of a typical commercially insured population is admitted to the hospital in any given year, and about 8 percent of those are readmitted within 90 days post-discharge.

Now suppose half of those readmissions were predictable enough to have merited close attention, and that this close attention prevents half of them from being readmitted, creating a 25 percent decline in total readmissions. That percentage reduction is quite impressive, that is, until one considers that a 25 percent reduction in readmissions—6 percent instead of 8 percent—equates to a 2 percent reduction in total admissions.

Since hospital expense constitutes half your spending, that 2 percent of hospital expense yields a 1 percent reduction in medical expense. This is barely enough to cover a PCMH's extra direct, visible fees.

And keep in mind that even if they offset the direct PCMH fees, those savings may offset only a small fraction of the extra medical claims expense that extra physician visits generate through extra prescriptions, referrals, and testing. The North Carolina Medicaid PCMH debacle shows how the hidden costs of care-begetting-care dwarfs the small extra monthly fee. This will be the subject of the next section.

4. **More PCP supervision of care, combined with an electronic medical record, will prevent redundant or unnecessary referrals and resource use.**
The increasing complexity of medicine precludes any return to the Marcus Welby days of a single doctor handling all care for an individual or family. It's not just the increased requirement of keeping up to date on advances; it's finances, as well.

For instance: Al's sinus diagnosis required use of a nasal endoscope. Presumably any trained physician, along with anybody else who's seen the insides of enough noses, could recognize polyps through that scope. The constraint is not the medical training; it's the actual ownership of such a scope, which costs several thousand dollars and requires regular specialized maintenance. The economics make sense only for an ENT, who is going to use it regularly. But since the scope exists and allows for a diagnosis, Al's PCP couldn't have really declined to give him access to a specialist who had one.

No amount of extra payment to the PCP as part of a PCMH could change the PCP's decision to refer Al, unless the PCMH payment was high enough to justify the primary care physician buying a nasal endoscope. And if that were to happen, the PCP would find plenty of other noses to investigate and diagnose, since looking in someone's nose is separately billable as a procedure.

This is where the electronic medical record (EMR) comes in. EMRs are assumed to save so much money and increase quality so much that the government is subsidizing them. For instance, suppose that Al had already seen an ENT, and maybe even already had a diagnosis. However, suppose the ENT's notes were in the ENT's office but nowhere else. They wouldn't be any good if they weren't readily accessible, which means that absent an EMR, Al could get approved for a duplicate referral even if polyps had already been diagnosed.

It turns out that Al had indeed seen an ENT for something totally different (that would have self-resolved even without the visit, of course) five years earlier. The ENT had an EMR, and those notes were in the EMR, readily available to the PCP. Far from making the referral less likely, those EMR notes *facilitated* the PCP's referral, because Al had, in fact, been diagnosed with that deviated septum he originally thought was causing his hoarseness during the previous ENT visit. A deviated septum is one of those first-world diagnoses that many people blithely live with and that no one ever dies from that nonetheless would and did justify a referral.

Al's is not an isolated case. EMRs themselves do prevent some duplicate care and errors, since their functionality notifies users of some possible errors when certain entries are made and aggregates a great deal of data in one place. However, there is also evidence, published in March 2012 in *Health Affairs*, that EMRs may increase testing rather than reduce it.

5. **PCPs know what they are doing.**
   Though never stated explicitly, the assumption underlying the PCMH philosophy is that both the PCP and the nurse case manager—who often handles day-to-day patient interfaces—are highly competent. After all, you wouldn't place more responsibility for care in someone's hands unless that was the case. Yet there doesn't seem to be published evidence that this is the case. Companies that use CSCOEs for second opinions realize that they can trace most of the proposed unnecessary procedures back to an original PCP referral. And as you know, leading one of your employees into the "treatment trap" in this way can do serious harm to the patient—and cost you a small fortune.

6. **The PCP can help you control overall costs.**
   The old saw that "the doctor's pen is the most expensive medical instrument" is usually dragged out in healthcare conferences, and it has some truth to it. Along with my earlier suggestions to ask people to raise their hands if they've been the victim of medical errors or benefited from a wellness coach, the next time you are presenting on medical costs ask the audience members to raise their hands if they left the office *without* a prescription, referral, or order for more testing or therapy the last time they visited their primary care physician. It turns out that most people leave with at least one if not more of those items in their goodie bags, thus confirming that sometimes regular saws become old saws for very good reason.

   This was what happened in North Carolina. Its Medicaid costs per member climbed significantly as a result of all this primary care, with lots of those same goodie bag items (none of which even requires noticeable patient copays in the case of Medicaid), not being offset by lower admissions. Consequently, by 2010 (the last year for which the federal comparison is available) that state's costs/member were 24 to 40 percent higher in the Medicaid populations with access to a PCMH than neighboring states—despite the fact that the average cost of North Carolina health coverage in the commercial population, without PCMH access, was average for the region.

And if you're looking at overall costs, recall that the 10/80 rule applies with a vengeance to your health spending, even if you can't do much about it. On one side, a large chunk of your employee population never even goes to the doctor during a given year, yet you pay extra fees for them in a PCMH model. Then consider the other extreme—the most expensive cases you had last year. How many of those cases even involved the PCP to a noticeable degree? Many of them likely involved cancer or a rare disease. You'll also occasionally get a budget-busting preemie spending a month in the neonatal intensive care unit. Then there are the major procedures—bypasses, joint replacements, and transplants. Finally, add in the figurative and literal train wrecks. People in those situations would receive much of their care in an inpatient setting—a place where the "rounding" the PCP once did is now done by a hospitalist, making the PCP almost irrelevant during the period in which the most money is spent.*

The Difficulty of Measuring Outcomes and Some Advice for Doing That

Models where physicians are salaried may indeed generate better outcomes when supported by case managers and electronic medical records. The experience at Geisinger suggests this—albeit on a

---

* It's true that a PCMH model includes embedded case managers who monitor and assist the PCPs following discharge in these cases. And those case managers provide a valuable service to the members. However, they only rarely provide enough medical insight to prevent overutilization. And be careful what you ask for because you just might get it. When North Carolina switched to a medical home, they replaced respiratory therapists who "rounded" on asthmatic children offering, well, respiratory therapy, with case managers who only rarely even visited the children. And not only are those case managers not licensed or authorized to provide respiratory therapy, but most don't even carry a stethoscope. Try managing someone's asthma without a stethoscope.

Medicare population—but in most other cases, the data supports the logic. The most favorable outcomes on non-Medicare populations turn out to be quite flawed. One would also have thought that Medicaid, which would presumably have had worse initial access than a commercial population, would have been a ripe target for cost savings. Yet the cost of extra access in North Carolina seems to have overwhelmed the benefits even when the initial access level was much lower than in a commercial population such as yours.

North Carolina's Medicaid program outcomes were easy to measure, because a great deal of data is collected on state Medicaid programs. However, private-sector programs of the type you will be offered are difficult to measure; there are too many moving parts. And PCMH model proponents have been consistently scaling back expectations for savings. A brief look at this chart shows why measurement is so hard, yet cost increases so likely.

Initiative	Your Exposure
Disease Management	Vendor fee
Wellness	Vendor fee + participation incentives
Biometric Screens	Vendor fee + participation incentives + follow-up diagnostic tests + false positives
PCMH	Additional PCP fees + whatever the PCP orders or prescribes + whoever he refers to + whatever she does

The Difference between a Regular PCP and a PCMH May Be in the Billing

A large number of physicians would claim that they already do much of what a PCMH requires on their own, for example, providing after-hours availability of nurses to handle ongoing issues via the phone to avoid emergency admissions.

Indeed, *Family Practice Management*, the official journal of the American Academy of Family Physicians, published an article in November 2009 entitled "10 Steps to a Medical Home." Author

(continued)

(Continued)

Anton Kuzel recommended that practices that want to become medical homes "start with steps that increase practice revenue." Specifically, he advises billing the insurers for more things that the practice already does and simply hasn't been billing for. Our view: It is a rare worthwhile innovation in healthcare delivery that starts with charging more without doing more simply by filing claims forms more strategically. And if a practice already is doing more and providing PCMH-type management, what other leverage in managing patients is worth your paying for?

The article goes on to say that the extra revenue from this added billing will give physicians the money to hire case managers and take other steps to become a medical home, begging the question: Why just start with steps that increase practice revenue? Why not just end with those steps, too? In any other business, you invest in costs to add revenues. Here the recommendation is to invest in revenues to add costs. Why not use the extra revenue from upcoding to invest in your kids' tuition or a Boston Whaler?

If, indeed, these organizations are doing what they are supposed to be doing, the higher costs of operating the model will be offset by reductions in the following areas, which can easily be measured simply by counting their frequency:

- Emergency room and urgent care visits
- Admissions
- Specialist referrals
- Day surgeries
- High-cost diagnostics such as MRIs and other scans
- Outlier cases—the number of cases triggering the attachment point on your stop-loss policy

Note that reduction in readmissions is not on this list. Readmissions are a small percentage of total admissions in a working-age population such as yours. They receive extra attention because the federal authorities have decided to focus on them in yet another attempt to redirect the market to something they consider a worthy goal (as they did when reimbursing states extra to implement North Carolina-type medical home models and as they do with electronic medical records). In any event, readmissions would already be counted in the preceding bulleted list, since they're captured in both the overall reduction in admissions and the outlier case tally.

Action Steps

Your action steps here are quite simple, and boil down to two simple rules:

Rule One: Stay out of PCMHs forever and ACOs for now.

Rule Two: See Rule One.

If you do think about getting involved in these models, start by developing that dashboard tallying those categories across your entire organization. Keep track going forward, and if you have the data, go back a few years to discern the long-term direction of these categories. Then, if you do ever get involved in these organizations, you can see if the new model inflects that preexisting direction.

Because this dashboard is the correct way to measure, naturally most organizations selling you those programs won't measure this way. Instead, they'll employ classic vendor tricks, such as counting only your previously identified chronically ill employees or complex cases (and conveniently not counting the ones who *become* chronic after the program starts by having a heart attack or other high-cost event); measuring outcomes versus some mythical inflationary trend calculation; and/or enrolling only people motivated enough to want to participate. *Why Nobody Believes the Numbers* describes why these techniques overstate or misstate impact. It's enough for your purposes just to know that these tricks exist. Read all proposals, contracts, and outcomes reports carefully to make sure they don't appear.

Despite all the warnings, we'd like to close on a high note. For the record, many PCPs are competent, dedicated professionals, whether or not they are being paid extra to be in a PCMH. I use my PCP because I know he will not refer me to a cut-happy or test-happy specialist. (By contrast, Al says he uses his because she is nearby, available, personable, and—as the sinus story shows—highly responsive. As to getting his diagnoses and referrals right, he is "confident that someday the law of averages will catch up to her.")

Part II

Mostly Good News

Chapter 7

The Company-Sponsored Centers of Excellence Model

Y ou no doubt noticed two things about Part I:

1. *Cracking Health Costs* is a real potboiler, at least by the standards of books on health benefit administration, with dramatic, dishonest, expensive and/or potentially dangerous misuses of your money exposed on every page.
2. We've told you plenty of things not to do, but very little *to* do.

Part II is the opposite. There's very little drama from here on, so if you're reading *Cracking Health Costs* for the titillation, you should probably put it back on the shelf and resume reading something more titillating, like the back of a cereal box. We've done our exposing for the most part, and now it's time for the boring advice to show you ways to change your health benefit for the better. Boring, yes . . . but very useful, and this is a how-to book even if the first six chapters might have been more how-not-to. These next four chapters describe those rarest of rarities: initiatives that reduce health spending while saving employees money, improving outcomes, and raising productivity.

One way to achieve this is to establish direct contracts between employers and clinics and hospitals that have achieved outstanding levels of success in managing the care for the very sickest members of your workforce. We refer to these organizations as "Company-Sponsored Centers of Excellence" (CSCOEs), to specifically distinguish them from marketing-oriented models where a well-known hospital anchors a local network using the (often self-designated) moniker of "center of excellence." While *Cracking Health Costs* does not endorse, this chapter does suggest names. But all suggested names are purely merit-based. In the development of this list, no compensation was required, no promotional considerations were exchanged, and no animals were harmed.

The pace of companies announcing new CSCOE programs and/or covering more procedures is increasing. One is retail giant Walmart, which we'll reference throughout this chapter—both because I know it well as my former employer, and because Walmart is the leader in adopting CSCOEs. Nonetheless, you don't have to be the largest employer in the United States to follow suit. In fact, quite the opposite is true: any company with a self-insured health benefit can utilize this approach. (Smaller companies tend to be in local business health coalitions, which can sometimes handle this type of contracting for groups of their members cost-effectively. The economics are the same regardless of size. Smaller companies will see more "bouncing" year to year, but over 10 years a company with 1,000 employees should have the same experience as a company with 10,000 employees has in one year.)

One reason for this increase is that unnecessary procedures are also on the rise. Consider angioplasties. About 250,000 bypasses were done annually before angioplasties were introduced several decades ago. This new procedure was hailed as a much less invasive, far less expensive alternative to bypass, with pundits predicting they would replace as many as half of all bypasses. Fast-forward to the most recent data: about 1.1 million angioplasties are performed today, but seemingly none have replaced bypasses—of which more than 400,000 are now performed. All of this is despite substantial improvements in drug and diet therapy over this period, which should have replaced both, to a large degree.

Heart procedures are just one of the many overutilized interventions that have created the CSCOE movement. My extensive role in this arena—combined with the fact that my blog, www.cracking-healthcosts.com, often chronicles these types of programs—makes me the go-to guy for inquiries about it. This is why I feel that a question-and-answer format probably works best to describe it—since I've answered the same questions so many times.

Q: Why the push today for CSCOEs?
A: Recall from Chapter 1's myth/fact on the 10/80 rule that only a small percentage of this 10 percent can be addressed. This chapter is about how you would address that small percentage. Even if it's 2 percent of people, which it probably is, that 2 percent accounts for a disproportionate chunk of costs.

This small group of employees and covered family member who spend this disproportionate share of the total dollars is called the "outlier population." Partly because more of these outliers would simply have died previously, the cost associated with them has been growing rapidly in the past 15 years. It's driven by significant but costly advances in treatment modalities, creating $3.5-million cancer cases, and $800,000 costs per case for ventricular assist devices. Further, a single transplant today can cost nearly $2 million over five or six years. (The much lower—though still high—transplant costs listed later in this chapter cover only the transplant episode itself and exclude long-term maintenance and the possibility of rejection and complications.)

Q: What are the traits of the outlier group indicated for CSCOEs?

A: These outliers typically have multiple illnesses and are seeing multiple specialists and are also often in the middle of an episode of acute care. Moreover, my experience shows that fully 10 to 20 percent of them have been misdiagnosed. Further, experience shows that around 40 percent of outliers have either suboptimal or even completely misdirected treatment plans, as the transplant example I will describe illustrates and as the Mercy sidebar brings to life with the example of the first person flown to Springfield, Missouri, for spinal care. This high error rate on the outlier populations is driving companies to develop CSCOEs, due to the fact that remote carrier case management—often conducted on the telephone with incomplete and tardy information—is simply not equipped to manage these cases.

Let me give you an altogether-too-common example. A blocked artery can cause chest pain, or angina pectoris. In men, this condition is usually manifested in the upper left quadrant. Women sometimes have atypical angina that instead causes severe back pain. I've seen cases where women have been seriously misdiagnosed and scheduled for spine surgery when the underlying condition is a blocked artery, even though the last thing a woman with a blocked artery needs is spine surgery.

I spoke to a spine surgeon about that once. He confirmed that while it happens, if the cause of the back pain was a blocked artery, the woman should have been referred to a cardiologist. I thought, well sure—but still, it's not fate. If enough spine surgeons are aware of this possibility for common misdiagnosis, then they should rule it out *before* surgery—even if it means forgoing their surgery fee. Nonetheless, the chain of blame starts with the primary care doctor who failed to rule out angina before referring her to a back surgeon.

Almost certainly a patient complaining of back pain would receive a course of conservative therapy prior to any surgery recommendation, because most back pain resolves on its own over time. However, if this back pain is not a spontaneous, unique condition but rather a symptom of angina, it won't resolve on its own. Once the physician reaches that conclusion, he usually orders a number of imaging studies that will almost surely show abnormalities in the back. The reason is that most people with angina will be over 45, and most people over 45 have *something* in their spines that won't look right in an image. Even though spinal pain doesn't correlate closely with abnormal spinal images, the abnormalities are often assumed to be causing the pain, even if they are minor. At that point of that MRI interpretation, the patient will have typically fallen into the treatment trap that may well land her in completely counter-productive surgery. (That interpretation is why a spine surgeon is on somewhat solid ground for going forward with the surgery. It's not like the surgeon is making up the imaging.)

But CSCOE-level hospitals work completely differently. Their protocols call quite clearly for a "differential diagnosis" in these circumstances, for several reasons: because the misdiagnosis above is anticipated; because the physicians operate in teams, rather than making handoffs; and because certain types of surgery proposals, like this one, must pass through peer review. (Ironically, partly because of the peer review, most questionable surgeries in CSCOEs wouldn't even be proposed in the first place.)

Q: Why not just use local tertiary care hospitals—the facilities that handle the sickest patients—as centers of excellence?

A: Tertiary care centers in the United States vary hugely in their adherence to evidence-based medicine, coordinating care, diagnosing complex diagnoses correctly, and prescribing the optimal treatment plan (and, as the next chapter will show, in simply not harming the patient). When such variation exists, someone is right and someone is wrong. Some centers are already famous for getting it right, while others, though equally deserving, are much lesser known, which is why we are profiling two of the latter—Mercy Spine Center and Virginia Mason—in *Cracking Health Costs*. The sidebar at the end of this chapter, "What to Look for in a CSCOE" contains a list of factors you'll need to consider to learn whether a hospital is likely to handle these situations correctly. However, simply finding out whether you live in an area where surgeries are performed at a greater-than-average rate would be a start, and *The Dartmouth Atlas* can provide that information.

Q: Do senior executives support subsidizing employees to utilize CSCOEs?

A: When I explained this model to a senior executive at one of the world's largest companies, he observed that employees would get better quality care while spending less out of pocket—and the plan sponsor would save money, as well. He then asked why every company in the United States is not undertaking these programs. Alas, I had no good answer for him.

Q: What specifically would we be offering our employees through a CSCOE program?

A: Employees who have learned they need certain surgeries may have the option of traveling (along with a caregiver) to a CSCOE, both to cover a second opinion and then, if needed, for the surgery itself. Recognizing that patients are being flown in and housed, these CSCOEs, as described in the Mercy sidebar, are set up to compress whatever evaluation and care is needed into a short timeframe. Your company typically would cover all expenses for those trips as well as any copays. Each company can decide this for itself, but I recommend full coverage of out-of-pocket expenses. This is the simplest approach and sends the clearest, most positive message to employees. Adding a lot of asterisks will diminish morale, increase communication complexity, and make only a modest difference in the total amount the company spends on outliers versus simply covering all the out-of-pocket expenses.

Q: Which hospitals are recommended for CSCOE programs?

A: Any hospital that meets the criteria in the sidebar at the end of the chapter can become a CSCOE. Walmart uses the Cleveland Clinic (Cleveland, Ohio); Geisinger Medical Center (Danville, Pennsylvania); Mayo Clinics (Rochester, Minnesota; Scottsdale, Arizona; and Jacksonville, Florida); St. John's Mercy Hospital (Springfield, Missouri); Scott & White Memorial Hospital (Temple, Texas); and Virginia Mason Medical Center (Seattle, Washington). This list is not exclusive. For instance, Pepsi has set up Johns Hopkins as a CSCOE.

Is Mercy's Spine Center the Best Orthopedic Program You've Never Heard Of?

I'd like to take you into one of these hospitals, Mercy's Spine Center in Springfield, Missouri, to bring the surgery-avoidance and error-avoidance cultures to life. You can use Google and find that these folks have won all sorts of awards, but awards don't impress me. (Remember, Nebraska's wellness program won an award, too.) What impresses me is what hospitals do to win these awards, which, in the case of Mercy, is many things. We'll only cover a few.

And we'll start with a case study of the very first person to enter what we refer to as the CSCOE program. He has previously been told he needed a three-level anterior/posterior lumbar fusion, a complex procedure with poor outcomes in people such as himself who are 100 pounds overweight. He sees spine specialists in orthopedics, neurosurgery, pain management, and rehab. It is noted that he has psychological issues so he also sees a psychologist. Lead neurosurgeon Dr. Alan Scarrow gives the patient and his wife the team's recommendations: no surgery. Instead, weight loss and behavioral counseling are prescribed. The man starts to cry, as he had been told he would be paralyzed if he did not have the surgery (though ironically major mobility loss was much more likely if he did). The employer just saved $60,000. The patient just avoided a disaster.

As in that example, unlike almost every other spine center in the country, Mercy's tries not to perform surgery. Of every 100 patients referred to its spine center, a remarkable 80 end up getting conservative therapy. This is not without risk to Mercy's team. It can be embarrassing for a referring physician to tell a patient she needs surgery and then have the patient find out that she doesn't. There can also be pressure from the patient, who often wants his problem "fixed" and may have been told, "If you don't take care of degenerative back disease now it will cause problems later," when, in fact, the thing it's most likely to do is self-resolve. (This is complicated by the fact that patients do report almost immediate relief after some types of spine surgery . . . and the long-term problems don't start for years afterward.)

Mercy's "secrets" (in quotation marks because any hospital can do the same things, but almost none do) are teamwork and incentive alignment. A patient gets referred to a spine center—not a surgeon. That sets a different expectation and the fact that an entire team—including pain management specialists, a psychologist, and even chiropractors—is available means that patients who don't get surgery don't leave empty-handed. They are likely to receive nonsurgical therapy right on-site.

You might be thinking, with barely concealed sarcasm, "Yeah, right, all these doctors and nurses, trained to perform or assist with surgery and who, frankly, hate chiropractors, fell right into line." And you'd be correct. It was not a simple process to achieve staff buy-in to this new vision, and a lot of turnover ensued, but the result was a core group whose culture was aligned with the Mercy mission. Since then—as is often the case with cultures, good or bad—potential recruits self-select, allowing the culture to sustain itself.

Incentives are also more aligned with the culture. Unlike the models described elsewhere in *Cracking Health Costs*, Mercy's surgeons share proportionately in the rewards of doing fewer surgeries . . . and the costs of doing more. The concept of payment marching in lockstep with surgeries, where a gain for the surgeon is a loss for a risk-bearing hospital, doesn't exist here. The culture and payment structure rewards doing the right surgeries rather than doing the most surgeries. A surgeon doing the latter would be considered an outlier at Mercy, and not rewarded for what other hospitals might consider an excellent performance.

Don't take our word for this. One of the most controversial (a polite word for "unnecessary and self-serving, with poor outcomes") surgeries is lumbar fusion. In the United States as a whole, the number of these surgeries has increased 220 percent since 2003. However, at Mercy, the change is 0 percent. As Mercy's Dr. Scarrow observes, "Care that is not provided because it isn't necessary will always be cheaper than care provided at a discount."

When patients do need surgery, lumbar or otherwise, there are many important subtleties patients will—and won't—notice that

(continued)

(Continued)

contribute to better outcomes. For instance, ask lead orthopedic surgeon Dr. Fred McQueary what innovation has improved outcomes the most, and he won't cite fancy new equipment but rather a policy that patients must stop smoking for 30 days prior to their operations, confirmed by a preoperative urine test. The dispositive research findings underlying this policy are available to every hospital and payer . . . but a brief Google search will reveal that Mercy is one of only a few U.S. hospitals to turn this research into policy.

What patients won't notice is the standardization of supplies, instrumentation, and implants. Originally the spine team had eight implant vendors. This is typical of orthopedic practices, where every doctor wants his or her own toys, a desire that vendors milk to the point of naming implants after doctors, which enhances both egos and royalties. However, it also adds huge complexity and time as the surgical team must learn many sets of instrumentation. Shorter, and more routinized, surgeries reduce time under anesthesia, blood loss, and infection potential. Other steps that routinize additional aspects of the experience, such as preparation, also reduce infection potential. Surgeries are faster, safer, and—not coincidentally—less expensive, as you'll see when you procure bids for spinal CSCOEs.

And Mercy welcomes your bid request. Most of its business is on some kind of bid basis, which, as you can see from this sidebar, matches its business model perfectly. "Perfectly" is a very strong word but, as with much in *Cracking Health Costs*, the mantra is: don't take my word for it. Simply request its *Spine Center Physician Handbook* and you'll see how Mercy's culture matches its compensation structure and its business model.

Q: I don't recognize all those names. How did you select these CSCOEs you are recommending?

A: Others may seek somewhat different criteria, but the best approach is to start by looking for hospitals and clinics that meet the criteria for quality, ethics, incentives, and safety outlined in the end-of-chapter sidebar. I've found that the handful I've recommended get diagnoses and treatment plans right quite consistently. And while my experience is not data, I *saw* the people referred to CSCOEs both before and after as part of my job. I watched them improve. And, I had data as well: the rate of surgeries in the covered conditions fell quickly after different companies implemented these programs.

Let me give one example out of hundreds. An executive in a company I worked for called me and nervously asked for my help. He said he was doing poorly health-wise and inquired confidentially about going on long-term disability. He reported a variety of physical problems, felt terrible overall, and was going downhill fast. He had about four or five specific health issues and explained he was seeing multiple specialists. I suggested a trip to the Mayo Clinic.

This man called me some time later to thank me sincerely. He said he had received a very thorough examination by a team of doctors during his visit to the clinic. Further, he told me Mayo's doctors took him off all his prescription drugs, and prescribed four new ones. He felt like a new man in a matter of days. It turns out his local doctors had him on medicines whose interactions were toxic to him. However, because the combination was rare and not usually toxic, our pharmacy benefit manager's algorithm had not highlighted the toxicity potential. As a result of going to what later became a CSCOE, he was able to continue working for many more years. You may very well have employees in the same boat, as this kind of occurrence is far more common than most people think.

This is merely one example of exactly what we had hoped for by selecting those hospitals as CSCOEs: the expectation that the model of care in the CSCOE would identify and avoid over- and misutilization. While other hospitals may have equal or lower costs per procedure or test due to high volumes, consider what "Father of Management" Peter Drucker once said, not unlike Dr. Scarrow's observation in the sidebar: "Nothing is more wasteful than doing something efficiently that need not have been done at all." Not performing unnecessary surgeries—or in this case, not prescribing inappropriate drugs—saves more than just the cost. It also prevents a great deal of inconvenience and discomfort (read: lost productivity) for your employees.

There is also a likelihood, in the case of surgeries, that the procedure doesn't work; that there are complications (roughly 1 in 10 people who undergo inpatient surgeries have avoidable complications either during the hospital stay or after discharge); and/or that years of follow-up care will be required. Getting this right saves lives, too. In short, the best care for your outliers will be the most cost-effective, too.

The previous chapter cautions employers against racing into direct contracts with Accountable Care Organizations (ACOs). However, I would categorize many of the clinics I recommend contracting with as CSCOEs as "naturally occurring ACOs," that is, organizations that grew up using salaried physicians and a tradition of teamwork. Furthermore, the doctors in the clinics I recommend genuinely are accountable—a crucial feature of a successful CSCOE even if it doesn't carry the "Accountable Care Organization" label, a label that correlates only loosely with genuine accountability. These clinics avoid incentivizing doctors to perform unnecessary procedures, and/or have an effective accountability mechanism in place that prevents this from happening.

By contrast, other hospitals that now layer an ACO-like structure on top of a more typical volume-based culture usually feature incentives for surgeons not to operate that are much more modest than the fees that they continue to receive for operating in those situations.

Incentives not to overtreat are a starting point in most of my recommendations of clinics as CSCOEs; however, we of course still want best-in-class performance for the procedures that are undertaken. That's why not every hospital in the centers network is contracted for all the covered procedures.

Q: Which major companies have implemented CSCOEs?

A: The concept of employers directly contracting with hospitals and clinics is nothing new. Companies like British Petroleum in America, Burger King, and Hershey were directly contracting with providers as early as the 1980s. The difference is the CSCOEs focus on quality rather than price. Some leading companies like Lowes, Walmart, Pepsi, and Boeing have established CSCOEs and announced it publicly, while others have taken this initiative but done so quietly. Many more are considering it today—and not just major companies but much smaller ones, too. Already, 5 percent of my clients have fewer than 2,000 employees, and some emerging CSCOE users are business health coalitions that welcome employers far smaller than that.

This Is Not One of Those Situations Where Size Matters

As you know, *Cracking Health Costs* does not make endorsements (a stance for which Wiley's attorneys are eternally grateful). I do, however, occasionally mention companies that can solve problems—and this is one of those instances. If you are too busy, too small, or feel you lack the expertise to set up your own CSCOE as this chapter recommends, there's an organization called BridgeHealth Medical that may fit your needs. The company's specific mission is to avoid unnecessary surgeries through timely employee education, while ensuring that necessary procedures are handled by surgeons who perform them the most often with the best outcomes. (Its network is not based on a unique data set; volume and outcomes data is technically available to anyone, just not in user-friendly formats.)

BridgeHealth contracts with a small, geographically dispersed network of top-rated hospitals throughout the United States. These facilities agree to all-inclusive case rates, which results in significant savings to your plan. Furthermore, when a member selects a BridgeHealth provider, he or she often learns about less invasive—and less costly—options.

Essentially, it's exactly what we are talking about in this chapter, scaled so that any size company can do it.

Q: Are companies really going to dictate where their employees go for care?

A: I get that question a lot. I usually reply that if your self-insured company uses a network now, then you're already dictating where your employees get care. This is just a special network to take care of your outliers' special needs. And you are not forcing them to the CSCOE; you are merely making the option available, using a very attractive financial model.

Q: Our regular network already includes name-brand hospitals, and our carrier also provides case management. Why not just use what already exists?

A: While regular preferred provider organizations can do a very good job providing access to care for things like newborn deliveries, office visits, broken ankles, and hernia repairs, they are not set up for the typically complex and hard-to-diagnose outlier illnesses. Case management is almost invariably done only following an acute event, and it might be too late to influence care choices by that time. And the selection of hospitals for the network is based largely on pricing, since their sales promotion is mostly predicated on the size of their discounts.

Q: Which procedures are covered and why?

A: To get on this list, the procedure must satisfy the following four criteria fairly well or three criteria very well. The ideal covered procedure would be common, expensive, often of dubious value, and often unnecessary. Consequently, some companies—for example, Walmart—started with transplants. These proved successful enough that the company recently expanded its program to cover heart and spinal procedures. Other employers have started with heart and valve surgery, orthopedic surgery, and spine surgery.

Second opinions by local surgeons are often worse than worthless. Any surgeon who overturns another's recommendation to have surgery will find that his own recommendations suddenly start getting over-turned. Further, there may be only one group doing a particular surgery in smaller communities—and who is going to invalidate his partner's recommendation to operate?

Second opinions alone may justify travel, even if the procedure itself is not particularly expensive. For instance, angioplasties are not expensive surgeries, and yet Chapter 5 describes their very frequent inappropriateness for stable angina. Those would definitely be worth offering CSCOE second opinions.

Q: How much can we expect to save?

A: Excluding transplants, which we will address separately, roughly 2.4 million of the procedures for which a CSCOE would be indicated are performed every year. Since few of them are done on minors (and the rate of retirees receiving these procedures is not dissimilar enough from the rate on working-age people to merit a complex calculation), figure that there are about 200 million working-age adults in the denominator. Dividing the first figure into the second reveals that about 1.2 percent of the relevant population is getting one of these procedures annually. So if you have 500 employees and 500 adult dependents, you pay for 12 of these procedures a year. The consensus of commentators is that at least half those surgeries are unnecessary. Hence, six people a year will directly benefit from surgery avoidance, while many of the other six will likely enjoy a much better outcome from the surgery they do undergo.

You may be thinking: I'm doing all this for 12 people a year? Yes, but consider the following. First, that number excludes transplants, and while this wouldn't add much to the number of people it would add enough to the cost to merit a separate discussion. Second, when you add all the related medical expenses to the surgery itself, you average about $50,000 per procedure. Third, that $50,000 does not account for lost work time and reduced productivity when people finally do return to work. Figure another very conservative $10,000 for that, making it a grand total of $60,000.

So for each of six people you save most of the $60,000—or $360,000 in total—by avoiding the surgery altogether (I say "most of" because you still have to pay for one trip*). Against that savings, you're making one trip for all 12 people plus a second trip for the 6 who end up getting the surgery. Subtract $5,000 per trip (including a companion), for 18 trips, or $90,000, from that savings to yield the net result: $270,000.

What have you done to get that $270,000 per 1,000 covered adults? You didn't cut benefits, raise copays, increase deductibles, or any of those other death-by-a-thousand-cuts that employers use to save on their health spending. Instead you did exactly the opposite: gave your employees access to the best treatment the country has to offer. Finally, this arithmetic is conservative; it doesn't consider that people who avoided these surgeries would have needed follow-up care, too.

In addition to those dollar savings, the impact on the employees is, at the risk of sounding like a credit card commercial, priceless. Not just on the grateful ones who avoided surgeries or had better surgical outcomes, but on the countless others to whom you are sending the message: we want you to have the best care.

Although it was an internal program, Walmart even put out a press release announcing the expansion of its CSCOE program. Focus on this quotation from Sally Welborn, senior vice president for global benefits:

---

* You also have to pay for long-term nonsurgical therapy, but our experience shows that follow-up therapy after surgeries costs a similar amount.

We devoted extensive time developing Centers of Excellence in order to improve the quality of care our associates receive. We have identified six renowned healthcare systems that meet the highest quality standards for heart, spine, and transplant surgery. Through these hospital systems, our associates will have no out-of-pocket expenses and a greater peace of mind knowing they are receiving exceptional care from a facility that specializes in the procedure they require.

Q: What about transplants?

A: All the figures below exclude corneas, which at $24,000 each are not included in many companies' CSCOE programs.

According to actuarial consulting firm Milliman USA, transplant spending spread over all covered people in the under-65 population would exceed $73/year (though that average consists of $0 in many years offset by a massive sum in a few other years). Excluding kidneys, which cost about $280,000 apiece and are basically a commodity surgery today, the average cost is around $700,000 for the full episode of care, though some cost as much as $2 million.

The good news is that there are only about 16,000 kidney transplants and maybe 14,000 other organ transplants in the under-65 population each year—a rate of about 1 per 8,000 people. This supports the comment that you would spend $0 in seven out of every eight years, if you cover 1,000 people including dependents.

That's all true enough, but the other way of looking at it is this: once every eight years, you will have a single procedure that will cost you (and your stop-loss carrier, which will claw it back from you over time—any stop-loss carrier not smart enough to figure that out would already have gone bankrupt) an amount equal to about 5 percent of your total health spending for that entire eighth year on your entire population if it's a kidney or up to 18 percent if it's anything else.

During my career (both running the health benefits for large companies and as a consultant), I've used CSCOEs to reduce the cost per transplant actually performed by about 20 percent and helped companies avoid roughly 40 percent of transplants altogether.

Yes, you read that right. About 40 percent of covered plan enrollees were originally told they needed a transplant, but were discovered to *not* need a transplant when sent to the top clinics in the United States.

And it's not like your employees will go away thinking, "My employer basically just denied me a transplant so that it could save money." The clinics I've used for CSCOEs do such a great job of explaining why patients don't really need a transplant that employees will direct any frustration at the physician who made the original (unnecessary) recommendation.

Q: It seems like there are other surgeries that could be covered. Isn't this list expandable even using the criteria you suggested?

A: Yes, there are several more candidates that I suggest investigating, notably joint replacements and possibly even bariatric surgeries. Conservative therapy has the potential to put off total joint replacement surgeries and other orthopedic surgeries for years or even permanently.[*] This is a case where everyone benefits from delays made possible through effective conservative care; artificial joints have a limited lifespan and second replacements ("revisions") often lead to lifetime disability. And while bariatric surgeries aren't expensive, the complication rate is very high and varies greatly by hospital. The cost of complications can vastly exceed the price of the surgery, not to mention the lost work time. Consequently, picking the right hospital has a huge impact on outcomes for the employee and your company.

Prostate surgeries are another candidate for CSCOE second opinions, as well as a perfect example of a supply-creates-demand paradigm. One San Francisco hospital, Mt. Zion, purchased a $2-million robot to assist with those surgeries. Soon, 19 other hospitals in the Bay Area followed suit. So now there is $40,000,000 worth of additional robotic prostate surgery equipment within roughly a 50-mile radius of Fishermen's Wharf, while the number of prostates with large numbers of aggressive malignant cells is remaining constant. Since insurers won't pay more for robotic surgeries, the hospitals have to make it up on volume. Within a few years, a good bet is that *The Dartmouth Atlas* will suddenly show very high rates of prostate surgeries in that area, aided

---

[*] See www.selfcarefirst.com. Employers and HMOs report substantial savings by avoiding orthopedic and spinal procedures using a specific type of conservative therapy. We have not reviewed their outcomes in detail but we would suggest gambling a click-through to take a look at their site.

by the fact that many men's prostates have inconsequential numbers or types of cancerous cells that will show up if one looks hard enough.

One might assume that at the very least—even if too many surgeries are performed—patients are getting better outcomes with the robots than without. Or are they? *Kaiser Health News* (March 19, 2012) reports no difference in outcomes between the robotic and nonrobotic surgeries. And according to the *New England Journal of Medicine* (July 18, 2012), it turns out that in men whose prostate cancer is localized, prostate surgeries—robotic or not—do absolutely nothing in the long term other than lead to more cases of incontinence and impotence.

And it looks like the same might be happening with robotic hysterectomies. The *New York Times* (February 26, 2013) reports a significant cost hike but no difference in outcomes . . . while at the same time there is general agreement that far too many women (about one in three) have their uteruses removed.

Q: What should we look for in a CSCOE?

A: Here are eight attributes of hospitals and clinics you should look for, or avoid, as a potential Company-Sponsored Center of Excellence:

1. The hospital or clinic should be fully integrated, meaning the doctors and hospital facilities are all part of the same organization.

2. The doctors, especially surgeons, are fully salaried, with no (or only minor) bonuses for doing more surgery. (Sometimes these bonuses are described as "productivity bonuses." Make sure that term is defined.)

3. The doctors should be accountable for getting the patients' diagnoses right, finding the safest and least invasive treatment to achieve the desired patient outcomes, and excellent patient outcomes.

4. Very few surgeons—even heart surgeons—track their patients for any length of time to observe their long-term outcomes, despite the fact that these are a critical input for a Continuous Quality Improvement process. Ensure that a potential CSCOE has a mechanism to do this.

5. Look for hospitals and clinics that are willing to provide global fees or other transparent prices.

6. Be careful of academic health systems. You should stay away from any hospital with a name that starts with the words "University of. . . ." (And, note that some hospitals are university-affiliated even without the moniker.) University-based health systems have three missions: research, education, and patient care—the first two of which often conflict with the third. Many of the worst cases I've seen of overtreatment and gross misdiagnoses have come from university health systems. Other hospitals have teaching programs, of course; the issue is determining the facility's main focus. Sometimes just reading the mission statement provides an answer to this question.

7. The hospitals should have a specific medical destination program, incorporating logistical elements (such as compressed time frames for evaluations) that anticipate people being flown in at your expense.

8. The hospitals should be nonprofit. The facts on this speak for themselves: in recent years, just about every publicized case of systemic inappropriate surgeries has come from for-profit hospitals.

Eureka: A Consulting Firm That Gets CSCOEs Right

Even Diogenes would have given up on this search, but I found one: a consulting firm that has done the CSCOE math . . . and now we work together. Chicago-based Laurus Strategies doesn't just get it right—they guarantee that if a solution doesn't bring value to your company, you shouldn't pay your consultant, or the solution (wellness) vendor.

"Today's large self-funded employers have much more opportunity to improve quality and reduce cost than they care to admit. And they can start getting it right tomorrow by being bold," says Mark Kendall of Laurus Strategies. "But they don't. Instead they do the easy thing: throw money at inept wellness initiatives that make them feel good."

Laurus's model, like this book, is based on facts rather than beliefs. They've done the risk factor math and the CSCOE math . . .

(Continued)

and CSCOEs win hands-down. "The healthcare delivery system and practice variations are driving healthcare cost increases. Therefore trying to control costs by reducing health risk factors will not solve the problem. The numbers simply don't add up, period.

"The right answer is exactly the opposite of wellness programs spending large sums to reduce long-term risks on an unmotivated population. Rather, a small percenage of our working population needs major interventions and is already highly motivated to find the best ones."

Addressing this issue is the Laurus transplant model, which offers a turnkey solution to employers to provide patients with access to world-class care at a fraction of the total expense of receiving care at lesser-qualified hospitals. "The lowest-priced transplant is usually the one that should be avoided because the hospital is trying to push volume," says Kendall. "About half the organ transplants for which our clients' employees have been scheduled turn out to be misguided and unnecessary. Our program doesn't just go after discounts on transplants but makes sure you don't get a transplant based on a misdiagnosis."

Laurus believes benefit managers should be challenged by their consultants to do something bold. "Implementing a simple change to your Summary Plan Description to incentivize or mandate an all-expense-paid on-site second opinion for your highest cost procedures can have a big payoff," says Kendall. "Communicate it wisely and stop paying for unnecessary transplants."

Just one avoided transplant will save you more money than a decade's worth of "biggest loser" contests.

Chapter 8

Hospital Safety: How to Get Your Employees Back to Work in One Piece

One day last year four benefits executives from one beachside community's leading employers visited their local hospital for a briefing and a tour. Collectively, these employers spent tens of millions of dollars paying hospital bills every year. Because these companies pay so much more per patient than Medicare or Medicaid does, their money allowed the hospital to develop state-of-the-art technology and enabled the renovation of an elegant lobby with gleaming marble floors. Some of these employers, like others across the country (possibly including you), spend more on health benefits than they earn in profits.

For all that investment, the four executives made exactly one request of this hospital: complete the annual Leapfrog Hospital Survey. A national nonprofit enterprise founded in 2000 by U.S. employers, the Leapfrog Survey collects data that's not available anywhere else on measures of greatest importance to purchasers. They gather information on everything from infection rates to mortality from certain procedures to the presence of management practices known to protect patients from unintended harm. The survey is free to hospitals and the findings are free to consumers. It takes about 40 to 80 hours of staff time for hospitals to complete the survey each year.

If this were any other vendor to whom these businesses paid more money than they earned in net after-tax profits, the four executives would have expected the red carpet treatment at their visit. Instead, they were greeted with a scolding. "It's just not reasonable of you to expect us to continue giving you the Leapfrog results every year in the future," a hospital vice president told them. "We are under a lot of pressure to report our quality to many sources, and we will have to put the priority on those paying our bills."

The reaction in the room was utter silence—in our imagination punctuated by the background sounds of the cascading 20-foot fountain set atop the cathedral ceiling in the lobby. It was Leapfrog's executive, Leah Binder, who finally broke the silence. "Just to let you know," she said, pointing to the visiting executives, "these are the guys paying your bills."

"Well, of course, and I mean no offense," replied the hospital leader, "but I'm talking about the health plans."

"Um, these are the guys paying the health plans," said Binder.

Binder recounts this in the introduction to a white paper published by the nonprofit healthcare think tank Altarum Institute (www.altarum .org) on employer strategies for purchasing hospital care entitled *Steering Employees Toward Safer Care: Employer Strategies for Attaining Safer, Higher-Quality Hospital Care for Employees and Their Families.*[1] She explains, "The hospital's [apparent] naiveté about the source of the health plan money was disconcerting. But what really shocked me was the naiveté of the employer executives in the room, who seemed sympathetic to the hospital." She points out these executives were anything but shrinking violets in their daily business outside the hospital, where they led successful businesses. But they turned into deer in the headlights in the face of hospital leadership, willing to tolerate vendor behavior that would be unthinkable for any other purchase. "Imagine an office supply purveyor refusing to spend a few hours answering a customer request for a report on the quality of their products. They wouldn't be scolding the customer for having the nerve to ask for such a thing. No office supply customer would put up with that," adds Binder.

Unfortunately, it's not just companies in quaint beach communities that put up with this kind of treatment from hospitals. It's you, too. Chances are that even though you're investing in wellness and disease management programs, you have no specific strategy to address hospital spending—beyond hoping to keep people out of them. (Check your days/1,000 to see how well that's working.) In fact, *Cracking Health Costs* may be the first time you've seen such a strategy appear in print.

Yet hospitals probably constitute about 50 percent of your overall healthcare spend. And, as we've seen in previous chapters, they try their hardest to increase that percentage by—among other things— investing in new equipment that they then often advertise directly to the public. They also increase that percentage, even without trying, through extending stays to address errors and infections that they themselves created.

We've already provided half the strategy to reduce that percentage: medical travel through use of CSCOEs. But what about the many hospital admissions that don't justify flying people out of town—people who may end up in unsafe hospitals right in town?

"Unsafe hospital practices may be one of the least publicized yet most modifiable aspects of healthcare quality," say the report's authors, Wendy Lynch and Brad Smith. "The magnitude of avoidable suffering, loss of life, and added cost is alarming." The Altarum report lays out options for managing purchasing summarized below, but notes that relatively few employers appear to go beyond the most modest action of publicly reporting hospital results.

Indeed, without the glare of market accountability, many hospitals deliver very poor safety and quality for the communities and patients they serve. According to an audit by Medicare's inspector general, one in four Medicare patients admitted to a hospital suffers some form of unintended harm. Few of us would get on a flight if we knew we had a one in four chance of getting harmed *en route*. Yet somehow, this caution doesn't carry over to the world of medicine. Over 180,000 people die in hospitals each year from errors, accidents, and infections.[2] The Institute of Medicine estimates one-third of healthcare is wasted—and a large portion of this comes from unneeded hospital procedures that result not only in high costs, but pain, disability, and even death for many patients.[3] And who do think is paying for this? You wouldn't put up with this error rate from your disease management vendor to whom you pay less than $4 per employee per month. Yet you accept it from your hospitals to which you pay $400 per employee per month.

Using a high-deductible plan might help control some other expenses. But nearly every inpatient stay exhausts the allowed annual deductible, saddling your company with the rest of the bill. That means even if your employees become adept at shopping for outpatient care, lab, radiology, and physician services, they will still have little or no incentive to shop for the most price-competitive hospital. Indeed, a disreputable, profit-maximizing Accountable Care Organization (ACO) could underprice primary and specialty physician care in order to generate referrals to affiliated hospitals, which then leverage that demand to inflate prices charged to plans and employers. (And if I can figure this strategy out, they can, too—which is one of the many reasons to tread carefully in this new environment.)

So here you have very high-priced suppliers producing a slipshod product . . . and yet your only strategy today is to try not to use them by instead using wellness programs that, as previous chapters showed, may create *more* provider interaction. I suspect the following are the barriers preventing you from being more assertive with provider organizations.

Barrier One: "I can't pretend to know more than the doctors and nurses." A medical degree carries an almost mystical cultural weight in our society, and even the most accomplished business leaders will balk at confronting doctors about how well they are running their hospital. This is probably the central unspoken reason so many employers act against their own obvious business interests by ignoring hospitals and favoring internally focused strategies that generate little or no friction with providers, such as "biggest loser" contests. Yet you don't have to know how to manage a hospital or perform brain surgery to demand the best outcomes at the right price from someone you're paying to provide a service. Most of us, business leaders or not, learn to be discerning consumers of products or services—even without any understanding whatsoever of how those goods are made. Few of us have any clue how a picture travels from the studio to our TV screens, but that doesn't prevent us from comparison-shopping for TVs. Hospitals need to be treated no differently.

Barrier Two: "I don't know how to evaluate the quality of a hospital." One of the problems in the past has been that you had no information to judge whether you were getting good results from the hospitals your employees are using. But it's ridiculously easy to do so nowadays. The hospitals are all scored with letter grades by Leapfrog Group based on their safety. An "A" hospital is much safer than a "C" hospital. However, do you recall from the previous chapter that while we can evaluate the experiences of patients who are operated upon, we cannot assess whether a hospital should have allowed a patient to receive said operation in the first place (hence, the CSCOE emphasis on procedure avoidance)? But for local hospitals and routine surgeries, Leapfrog is as good as it gets.

By way of background, Leapfrog was founded in 2000 by some frustrated large purchasers, including Boeing, General Motors, and General Electric. The system relies on employer members to pressure hospitals to publicly report to them on their rates of errors, infections, mortality from key procedures, and maternity care quality. Leapfrog publishes the results by hospital annually and makes them free to the public and usable by purchasers via their website: www.leapfroggroup.org.

In 2012, Leapfrog launched an additional initiative that every employer should be using immediately called the Hospital Safety Score—the aforementioned letter grade they assign to general hospitals to rate their patient safety. Leapfrog doesn't rely on voluntary reporting by the hospital to arrive at this score. Instead, it uses publicly available data to issue the grade. Employers and the public can search letter grades on the website www.hospitalsafetyscore.org or download the free app on Android devices or iPhones. The *Wall Street Journal* (December 17, 2012) named the Hospital Safety Score as one of the top 10 ways patients got treated better in 2012 than in 2011.

Don't Rely on *U.S. News & World Report* Rankings

You might be wondering why, when selecting hospitals for the CSCOE program or in this chapter, we didn't rely or even refer to the well-established *U.S. News* rankings. Perhaps the best answer to that question would come from Paul Levy, who himself ran a hospital—Boston's Beth Israel Deaconess—from 2002 to 2011. No sour grapes here—Mr. Levy's hospital usually scored quite well in the rankings. Even so, his blog, www.runningahospital.blogspot .com, cites observations that we found persuasive on the question of the ranking's trustworthiness:

◆ 32.5 percent of the score is based on reputation—which poses a problem several ways. First, large hospitals will inevitably score higher, since more of the survey's respondents will have heard of them, may have trained under their doctors (the high-ranked hospitals overrepresent academic medical centers), or have read papers/seen presentations by their doctors. Second, the separation between high and low reputation scores, combined with the 32.5 percent weighting of reputation category, means that reputation drives the rankings. Third, this methodology creates a self-fulfilling

(continued)

(Continued)

prophecy where high rankings enhance reputations, and then respondents subsequently rank hospitals high on reputation because they rank high in the rankings.

- ◆ The whole concept of using physician respondents is flawed. How can busy physicians possibly know what is going on at 4,000-plus other hospitals elsewhere in the country?
- ◆ Only 5 percent of the score is based on safety. Using pulmonology as an example, the top two hospitals have great reputations but low safety scores. The first hospital with a superior safety score is number 21 on the list. Where would you rather be admitted: a hospital with a great reputation among people who've almost certainly never been patients in it, or a hospital with a great patient safety score?

One thing that's tough to argue with—the ranking site is a terrific place to look at ads. Try visiting the www.usnews.com/besthospitals site and, at least as of this writing, the first thing you see is an ad . . . and there are plenty more where that one came from.

Barrier Three: "My health plan handles my relationship with hospitals. I don't need to get involved." There is no question that without health plans, you would have to work directly with individual doctors and hospitals and negotiate your own deals on price and quality of care—an unmanageable operational burden for many (though some are doing it). Yet you should resist the temptation to delegate 100 percent of the important purchasing decisions to health plans—and here's why: they have a strong interest in maintaining productive relationships with hospitals and doctors to satisfy their entire book of business—all of the companies they represent, not just yours. And, as noted in previous chapters, they want to be able to advertise the great prices they've negotiated. A health plan with a reputation for making hospitals jump through quality hoops is not going to find many willing to give it a great price.

By contrast, your benefits program should have just one priority: the best care at the best price for employees. Employers who rely on health plans to inform them of the quality of care their employees receive will not always get the information they need. And even when they get that information, they will often discover that the plan doesn't accommodate changes to benefits packages or hospital contracts to leverage purchasing power. Rarely will a health plan agree to eliminate a hospital from its network on the advice of even its largest purchaser client.

Barrier Four: "My business doesn't have enough purchasing leverage to influence hospitals." It is true that even the largest companies cannot materially influence market share for many hospitals. Most hospitals are focused on Medicare/Medicaid demands, since together those programs pay for at least a third of their patients. Nonetheless, hospitals do depend on employers because they charge them much more for services than they can get from the public programs—as much as three or four times more for each patient. Hospitals openly acknowledge this as something they call "cost-shifting." The good news about you paying that much money is that hospitals worry more about losing market share among the commercially insured populations than they do for Medicare populations. As a result, you have more leverage than might be reflected in your sheer number of covered lives.

You can achieve the greatest leverage if you join with other employers in your market to negotiate deals and make demands of hospitals on behalf of your total covered lives. Though this can obviously work in theory, it requires that all the participating purchasers take action to affect the market share of local hospitals. See barriers 1, 2, and 3 for why this strategy often doesn't have enough teeth behind it to be as effective as it could be. This is what business coalitions on health are supposed to do, yet they often don't get adequate consensus and support, even from businesses that have paid for memberships to utilize their market power for major group negotiations.

You Don't Become a Leapfrog Top Hospital by Accident

Not all hospital rating systems are created equal. As Paul Levy describes them, most hospital ratings systems are a self-perpetuating, reputation-maintaining closed feedback loop, where doctors are asked to rate hospitals based on reputation. If they're not familiar with a hospital on the list, why not just go with how other doctors rate them? Following the hospital rating crowd, however, does little to elevate organizations that are actively challenging the status quo in health care delivery—organizations such as Virginia Mason.

Recognition from The Leapfrog Group is one force that helps balance the hospital ranking scales. Virginia Mason has received the organization's Top Hospital honor every year since the program's inception, one of only two hospitals nationwide to do so. Everything from the quality of medical procedures to computer order systems to hospital safety are scrutinized and scored. The data are intended to help consumers make healthcare decisions based on proven safety measures and medical outcomes—better decision points than reputation alone.

Employers and purchasers of healthcare have taken notice of Virginia Mason and its accolades for very good reasons. Here are just a few examples of how Virginia Mason has achieved unique breakthroughs in healthcare delivery:

◆ All Virginia Mason staff members are empowered to "stop the line" at the first sign of a potential error in patient care. No one knew if staff members would be willing to do this, but they have—more than 35,000 times since 2002.

◆ Virginia Mason's nurses redesigned the flow of care, working in teams to cover clusters of neighboring hospital rooms. Instead of rushing to treat patients scattered throughout a large hospital unit, nurses and technicians stay close to patients' bedsides. Nurses who once averaged 10,000 steps on duty each day now take only about 1,200.

◆ Primary care providers are often seen as the quarterbacks of healthcare, and yet the daily avalanche of data entry, paperwork, and e-mail threatens their ability to focus on patients. Virginia Mason created primary care flow stations where physicians and medical assistants meet throughout the day, knocking out the side work in smaller batches. Work done in flow serves patients faster, eliminates time-consuming phone calls, enables physicians to see more patients, and increases job satisfaction by getting clinic staff home in time for dinner.

◆ The Virginia Mason Breast Clinic did away with the agonizing wait for patients needing an appointment or hoping to get test results. After a focused revamp of services, not only can 98 percent of patients get a Breast Clinic visit within 24 hours, the time between a patient's first call and receiving a diagnosis was shortened from the industry average of 20 days to 3 days.

◆ Before medical center renovations are undertaken, a replica of the future space is temporarily constructed on a vacant floor maintained specifically for this purpose. Employees on that floor are invited to perform a dry run version of their jobs to provide feedback on how the proposed design will function in a real-life work setting. Their feedback is used to adapt construction plans to their needs.

Action Steps

With those barriers taken into account, here are six things you can do.

First, determine your frequent lower-cost procedures. You're doing something similar to this for infrequent high-cost procedures through CSCOEs. You now need a solution for your frequent low-cost procedures. Imagine the same logic of CSCOEs applied to local networks. The first step is discerning which procedures fit this category.

Second, review those procedures against the Leapfrog scores at the hospitals in which those procedures were done. Many hospitals report total Leapfrog scores, and all have Hospital Safety Scores (HSS), since those are calculated off publicly reported data. It's a fairly safe assumption that those that do not report the total scores but have low HSS would have low total scores. You can then match the procedures to the hospitals to see how much risk you are taking on. You can also check Leapfrog ratings on mortality, electronic prescribing, length of stay, and other indicators if the hospital voluntarily reports them at www.leapfroggroup.org.

Third, do some simple arithmetic to see what these lower scores are costing you and, through greater chance of harm, your employees. The Leapfrog website allows you to download a free simple spreadsheet that directionally (though not precisely) lets you determine how much extra you paid because your employees went to hospitals more likely to harm them. I say "though not precisely" because there are a lot of moving parts in hospital spending, as well as in the components of the Leapfrog score. But the overall message will be clear: errors here, just like in your base business, cost a lot of money.

Fourth, *tell* your employees which hospitals are better than which other ones. Your organization is vigilant about potential safety hazards in the workplace and no doubt trains your staff in how to avoid them. Some companies have a nobler purpose in doing so, but injuries cost all companies money. Likewise, a hospital that earns a low safety score is considerably riskier to employees in terms of infections, medication errors, and—my favorite—objects left in your body after surgery (see the aptly named website www.NoThingleftbehind.org). Employers pay for these errors, both in direct health claims and in lost productivity and disability claims. Training your staff in this case is fairly simple: it means suggesting which hospitals to avoid and which to use.

Fifth, just as with CSCOEs, nudge employees financially toward the higher quality hospitals. You have the precedent with CSCOEs to structure benefits packages to reduce copays for using hospitals that perform well on Leapfrog surveys and possibly increase copays for the others. As the Altarum paper recounts, Maine state employees have their $250 inpatient copay waived if they use high-performing hospitals—a simple move that has driven significant quality improvement there. These tactics are not strategically complex and will demonstrate significant cost savings. (You can also remove hospitals from your network altogether, of course, however; unless you are in a dense urban area with plenty of alternatives, you might get a lot of pushback.)

Sixth, let the hospitals know you've done this. You don't have to confront hospitals and demand improvements. Rather, just let them know you support Leapfrog and are tweaking your benefits design. Presumably, given the profitability that they extract from you and other businesses whom they feel you might talk to, some will respond by trying to improve their scores. You can also ask the hospitals to respond to the Leapfrog Survey if they have failed to do so. And, unlike our friends in the beachfront community, assert your expectations as a purchaser when the hospital complains that this is asking too much. (A hospital that won't provide information to Leapfrog might be like a homebuyer during the housing boom who insisted on a "no-doc" loan . . . and now we know why.) If they have an issue with the scores or the scoring methodology, just point them to Leapfrog; they can raise any concerns with them.

In summary, you can—without much difficulty—address the rampant waste, unnecessary procedures, accidents, errors, injuries, and poor quality that are all too common in hospitals. You can tweak benefits packages, inform employees of hospital performance, and let the hospitals know you're doing this. As hospital services consume a growing percentage of your healthcare spend, these strategies become increasingly critical.

And perhaps the most critical point: don't do this alone. Get your counterparts elsewhere to do the same thing. The informational issues in particular should be easy for others to implement—and the more companies doing it, the better.

Chapter 9

Real Care Coordination: The Only Other Way to Save Money

D ivision of labor was born more than a century ago when Henry Ford segregated job functions so that each laborer performed the same step repetitively. Each worker operated in a silo, knowing only his (no "her" back then, on the factory floor) role. In fact, it was believed that workers should not be confused by seeing or understanding the functions performed down the line, because all that could do was slow production. Amazing efficiencies resulted, and the River Rouge plant became the model for manufacturing everywhere.

That was 1908, and it was a factory, not a call center, but most of the health insurance industry still does the Henry Ford thing today, isolating customer service, eligibility, utilization management, and complex case management as separate, vertical siloes. Alas, division of labor turns out to have been far better suited to making black Model Ts than to managing complex health benefits.

For the latter, *Why Nobody Believes the Numbers* helped popularize the opposite model, which utilizes a horizontal, cross-functional team approach to benefits management, because Al discovered that this was the only model that actually delivered savings (as opposed to *saying* that savings were delivered, which is the industry standard). Al portrayed Quantum Health as an excellent example of this, and the Quantum Health model, which we will call the "care coordination model" in order to avoid plugging a particular vendor, has subsequently become even more popular as a way to control benefits expense. (A full list of vendors providing true care coordination is provided at www.dismgmt.com, under Gold Standard. It's not a list that, as of this writing, will take a long time to read.)

What happened next was quite predictable: for showing companies how to reduce their healthcare cost by several percentage points; Al got in a lot of trouble.

Why? Because, remember how Nordstrom's used to have piano players in its lobbies? And the company's reputation for customer service was stellar enough that the urban legend about it refunding a customer for tires, even though it doesn't sell tires, was widely believed? (By the way, the backstory of that tire rumor is worth a Google search. Like many urban legends, it actually contains a molecule of truth.) Several department stores then put piano players in their lobbies, thinking that would make them like Nordstrom's.

The same exact thing happened with the care coordination model. Carriers would adopt a stray tidbit of it and then say, "We use the care coordination model." Usually their definition of care coordination was simply that someone calling member services with a question sounding like a disease management question would be transferred to disease management—the equivalent of the piano in the lobby.

While helpful, that misses about 99 percent of the care coordination model, which integrates all of the following elements into one cohesive process:

- ◆ Customer service for all benefits issues including eligibility, coverage, and claims
- ◆ Provider services
- ◆ Utilization management, including:
  - Precertification
  - Concurrent inpatient review/case management
  - Retrospective review
- ◆ Case management
- ◆ Disease management
- ◆ Wellness programs (for employers that insist)

In most employer-sponsored benefit plans, these functions would be spread across at least vendors or departments. Customer service calls related to these functions would go to several different toll-free numbers and call centers, and the data related to these functions and service calls would reside in different IT systems. This is even the case for most carriers that address all of these functions, and is certainly the case for self-insured employers that build their own benefit plan vendor structure, attempting to select best of breed vendors in each area. Even when one vendor, such as an insurance carrier, provides all of these functions, they are almost always housed in separate operating divisions in separate calls centers and IT systems. In short, the different business functions operate as separate, vertical silos.

As an example, in many if not most, insurance carrier operations the nurses who provide utilization management or complex case management are housed in different divisions from customer service functions related to eligibility, benefits, and claims. Often they are in different cities—sometimes even in different countries. Almost invariably the nurses cannot determine or quote benefits, and the customer service agents cannot discuss clinical issues. Even when these service roles are co-located in a regional operations center, the business functions are intentionally kept unconnected.

In an example that is probably more the rule than the exception, the nurses in the regional operations center of one major carrier were on the second floor, while the customer service agents (CSAs) were on the first. The CSAs were strictly forbidden from interacting with the nurses other than personal conversation in the lunchroom; neither was allowed to go onto the other floor, sort of like Ford workers not being allowed down the line. The reason, of course, is to maintain focus and operational efficiency *within* each role, which certainly reduced operating cost. The good news is that this operational efficiency allows such vendors to keep their administrative costs, which they pass on to employers, as low as possible.

Unfortunately, that approach addressed the wrong variable: administrative costs generally represent about 10 percent of total health plan costs. Managing the other 90 percent—the actual health claims cost—in the most efficient manner is more important. For instance, reduce administrative expenses by 5 percent and your total cost falls 0.5 percent (5 percent × 10 percent). Reduce medical spending by 5 percent and your total cost falls 4.5 percent—nine times as much.

The care coordination model replaces silos with a horizontal structure in which the functions operate as one cohesive business process and service offering. While this may not minimize the administrative fee, this approach should control overall cost much better. This integrated service approach achieves greater levels of care coordination, avoiding duplication, delays, and other waste. As you've seen, we are quite skeptical of most ways to separate you from your money, but this is not that situation: true coordinated care significantly reduces cost in a sustained manner while also attaining high levels of employee satisfaction. The downside is, like anything worth doing (and unlike most things vendors and consultants pitch), it is a major undertaking, which is why more companies don't do it despite the savings potential. A number of different functions—currently housed across numerous vendors—must be carved out from these vendors and reassembled under one vendor.

The success of this model and the industrywide movement toward achieving better coordination of care and accountability-based reimbursement structures has sent many vendors and carriers scurrying in this direction. Wellness and disease management vendors are broadening their services and expanding into the other functions previously listed. Third-party administrators, who historically specialized in claims processing and administrative customer service, are expanding the health management functions and attempting to integrate these processes. Insurance carriers are trying to create integrated benefit plan models in an attempt to break down the traditional vertical silos in their organizations, with the hope of achieving greater coordination of care and a resulting reduction in claims cost.

We believe this is not just a fad, but rather a sea change in the way health benefits are delivered. This trend coincides with the emerging movement toward Accountable Care Organizations (ACOs), which—as outlined in Chapter 6—we advise employers to monitor but not to jump into too soon. Think of the care coordination model as an ACO run for employers rather than by providers. No need to worry about conflicts of interest or your ACO needing to perform a certain number of procedures to cover the acquisition costs of a physician practice they just bought in a bidding war. And no worry about tying your fortunes to one ACO, which may come to dominate your metropolitan area and steal your negotiating leverage. Further, you can easily couple a Company-Sponsored Center of Excellence (CSCOE) to a care coordination model, much more so than to an ACO.

How to Select a Coordinated Care Vendor

Below we have put together a skeletal care coordination RFP. (As a self-insured employer, you may request an actual such RFP from me, to save yourselves the trouble of copying down these questions longhand, like our forefathers used to do before the dawn of the personal computer.) The questions are designed to help you distinguish real care coordination from a façade that many carriers and vendors use to create the appearance of an integrated model—perhaps co-locating discrete functions in one room—but where further analysis reveals that the underlying functions, roles, processes, and data systems have not fundamentally changed. This is like the early versions of Windows, which were just new interface screens designed to look like a Macintosh that sat on top of the underlying MS-DOS, which simply could not do many things that the Macintosh was designed from the ground up to do. I remember many infuriating hours trying to get my Windows PC to print, a function that was second nature as a built-for-purpose Mac. Same interface, different innards.

So it goes in a care coordination-based benefit plan. True coordination of care cannot be achieved without rewiring the underlying roles, processes, and technology.

Since our goal in this book is to provide tangible how-to steps, the remainder of this chapter will outline specific questions to ask when evaluating coordinated care vendors.

Question 1: "Which of the functions listed at the beginning of this chapter will be provided by you?"

We recommend that you also ask whether they provide each function in-house or through a subcontractor, and if in-house how many years they have been providing that function.

A vendor that has provided the function for only one to two years is trying to move into the care coordination space, but new enough at it

One Thing You Need to Do Right Now

Even if you aren't ready to move to a coordinated care model now, it's never too early to anticipate that move in your administrative services contract. In your next administrative services RFP, ask the respondents to list the functions with their *a la carte* prices and indicate that you may carve some of them out at a later date and ask what if anything the fee would be to do that.

That way, if and when you do move to care coordination, there can't be any fussing from your carrier when it loses the functions and, more important from its viewpoint, the revenue from those functions. The carve-out terms will be pre-negotiated in the contract. Care coordination adds some services but replaces others, and you don't want to pay twice for the replaced services by layering a vendor on top of your carrier.

that its growing pains will take place on your nickel. Similarly, a vendor providing functions through a subcontractor is a nonstarter. The whole point of the horizontal, cross-functional team approach is to avoid handoffs and missed connections. Outsourced functions will never be as seamless as effective care coordination generally requires.

Question 2: "Are all functions accessed by plan members (employees and dependents) and providers through a single-point service process—one toll-free number, website, and other access channels?"

For true care coordination to occur, virtually all questions and issues related to healthcare must go through a single point of patient service and flow into one data system. Many benefit plans have three or more toll-free numbers that patients must call for different functions.[*] The problem is that patients often don't know which number to call when, and when they do get three different pieces of the answer, they are not equipped to stitch together the overall solution. Often employees end up calling whatever number has the shortest wait time.

Question 3: "How fully integrated are member services, patient advocacy, and care management functions in the vendor's operation?"

These are three main competencies required for care coordination to occur. It's not enough for the calls and e-mails to go to one service center—in point of fact, the issues coming through those contacts must be resolvable through one process. If CSAs, patient advocates, and nurses performing different care management functions sit in the same building but operate in silos with disconnected workflows, care coordination will not occur. Generally, you should see that the people responsible for these roles and functions sit in close proximity to each other so as to encourage interaction and shared problem solving.

So begin by asking for a description of how these processes are integrated. Follow up with a site visit to witness the operation and see for yourself whether cross-functional service and problem solving are occurring. The key point is that most complex healthcare issues involve all three of the following:

---

[*] One such card has 13 phone numbers. Really. I can send it to you if you like. It's not even a card. At first it looks like a card, but there are so many numbers you need to unfold it to see them all, sort of like the credits at the end of *Rocky and Bullwinkle*.

1. Benefit questions (For example, what is covered? is this approved for payment?).
2. Patient advocacy (How do I do this?).
3. Care management (Is it medically necessary? What are my other options? Can you walk me through a decision process?).

And perhaps most important, these are definitely not three separate issues in the mind of the employee/patient—these collapse into one question: "How do I solve my problem?" A vendor can only move beyond providing information to providing solutions by doing all three seamlessly. Your site visit should reveal actual operational indicators of this cross-functionality. People will talk back and forth, calls will be warm-transferred, little huddles may be occurring as nurses and CSAs problem solve together.

A note about site visits and protected health information (PHI): We have heard that some health plans and vendors won't allow prospective clients to observe actual operations, citing PHI. There are ways to allow prospects to observe operations while protecting PHI and/or having visitors sign a confidentiality and PHI nondisclosure agreement. Each vendor has its own view of privacy law interpretation, but many vendors have been conducting site visits for years, so it is possible. Call us conspiracy theorists but we think falling back on privacy is an excuse for not wanting you to observe their operations, sort of like when a president cites "executive privilege" to avoid turning over tapes or DNA.

After your observation, you should ask to get employees representing several different functions and roles in one room to talk through some recent cases (without using names, of course). You should hear examples of cases flowing seamlessly across functions, and situations where two or three people had to be involved to figure out and execute the solution. Many of these employees will have worked at other healthcare companies. Since care coordination models are the exception and not the rule, it is likely that some employees will describe how this operation achieves cross-functional care coordination in ways their previous employers did not. You will also likely hear evidence that CSAs do much more than answer administrative questions; in a care coordination model, they are simultaneously the identification and intake point for clinical and patient advocacy needs. They, therefore, will talk about how to recognize issues and clinical questions they have learned to ask when prompted by their software (that you should also ask to see).

Question 4: "How many calls do your CSAs handle?"

A typical CSA is required to take 80 to 110 calls per day. This standard is strictly monitored and enforced. If a particular call goes long, the CSA may get an electronic tap on the shoulder. This policy is a hallmark of "providing information, not solutions." If this number is greater than 50, it is unlikely the CSAs are actually coordinating care. When a plan member calls, the initial question they ask is often not the real issue; the CSA must recognize the signals, probe deeper, and identify the root cause. Then and only then can problem solving begin, and that may require several outbound calls or discussion with nurses, the claims examiner, patient advocates, or other CSAs.

Speaking of which, you can also ask about the inbound/outbound call ratio. There should be an average of at least one outbound call for each inbound call. If the vendor doesn't know this number, or says their agents are so good they handle all or most issues with "one-call resolution," it is highly likely they are providing answers rather than solutions and are not truly coordinating care.

Question 5: "Explain the role-blending in your organization and give specific examples."

Another key indicator of cross-functional operational is role blending, such as whether nurses understand and can quote benefits and work on solving claims issues. In traditional benefit plans, nurses are not trained in these areas, under the belief that it is a distraction from their higher level clinical function. The IT system they use may not even show the data necessary to explain or problem solve claims issues. But in a care coordination model, the role of nurses is not to handle clinical issues but to solve patient problems.

Question 6: "Does the IT/data system reflect a horizontal coordination of care platform?"

First, all roles should be able to view all the relevant data allowed by HIPAA. Nurses and CSAs operating on different systems is an immediate red flag. This is surprisingly common because CSAs are often looking at the claims administration system, while nurses are looking at separate care management software. If separate systems are in use, attempts may have been made to transfer certain data elements across systems, but roles and processes are unlikely to have become cross-functional. Assuming a pure care coordination software platform is being utilized, the next question is whether all roles can see the plan coverage certificate, can access provider networks for provider lookup, and can see claim data and care management data.

Finally, when you ask for demonstration of the system, you should see specific examples of tools and functions that provide better coordination of care. This should include alerts when someone is not meeting a care objective as well as when a duplicate service is being requested. What tools are in place to provide alerts to CSAs and/or nurses that a patient needs follow-up? How can a complex issue be flagged for later audit or follow-up?

Question 7: "What specialized staff development methodologies do you use to foster care coordination?"

Since care coordination requires breaking down silos, role blending, and nontraditional handoffs, specialized training is almost certainly required. A vendor that has interfaced but not integrated the separate functions will likely describe separate training programs for each function but not a special process to make that final link to cross-functional operation. Many approaches can be taken, so we don't list specific ones; the key is that your vendor should be able to describe some plausible effort in this area.

Question 8: "What specialized preadmission, post-discharge, and transition-of-care programs are included in the vendor's program?"

Traditional benefit plans typically approach inpatient admissions as an "approve or deny" opportunity. Frequently, they review the clinical information submitted in a pre-notification and approve the admission for a certain number of days. After this number of days, they conduct concurrent review by asking the hospital to submit a clinical update and may approve additional days.

By contrast, in a care coordination model, the vendor still certifies each inpatient day for payment but also tries to coordinate the entire cycle of the inpatient event, beginning even before admission with a preadmission call to the patient and/or family. Rather than grant a certain number of days in advance, the program may ask for a clinical update from the hospital every day, so that all patient needs can be identified and coordinated. Following discharge, calls are made at certain intervals to ensure the patient understands the discharge instructions, is taking medication correctly and makes necessary follow-up arrangements. In evaluating potential vendors, you should ask the vendor to list all activities that they routine conduct along that continuum.

Question 9: "Are post-discharge care management and disease management integrated?"

In most cases, the answer is no, meaning that people who most need disease management may not get it for many weeks following discharge. Demand to know exactly how the handoff is made, or whether the same person who manages immediate post-discharge care handles the ongoing disease management, the mark of true care coordination.

Question 10: "How are people who did not just get discharged referred into programs?"

Whoever is managing care must be in the loop far earlier than in the traditional model. To get in the loop, special notification tools need to be in place. This might include, for instance, a method for requesting and receiving notifications from a primary care provider when they are referring the patient to a specialist. (You may provide an incentive in a preferred provider organization model to encourage patients to ensure you are notified.) It may also include an expanded list of prior authorizations or pre-notifications the benefit plan requires or requests from providers. A traditional plan, doing traditional care management, will only ask for pre-notification of inpatient stays and few other procedures, because all they are reviewing against is clinical criteria for approval or denial. Since this function is rarely fruitful in today's environment, most carriers expend little effort here. However, a care coordination vendor will want notification of as many procedures and high-cost diagnostics as possible, because every notification may reveal a duplicate, delayed, or uncoordinated service—even if it is medically necessary. An expanded list of pre-notifications might include:

- Inpatient admissions
- Outpatient surgery
- MRIs, MRAs, and PET scans
- Occupational therapy, physical therapy, and speech therapy
- Sleep studies
- Oncology treatment

Question 11: "What do you report on?"

All health plan vendors report regularly on the basics, telling you where your money went. In a care coordination-based benefit plan, different kinds of reporting are both possible and necessary, and the goal should be to identify *why* your money went to certain expenditures, and what management tactics can be deployed to change this.

You should ask potential vendors to provide samples of standard reporting. In addition to the basics, these reports should answer these six questions:

1. What percent of your plan members are engaged with a primary care provider?
2. What is the ratio of primary care to secondary specialist utilization in your book of business?
3. What information will be provided back to physicians regarding their patients?
4. What percent of the total population do you talk to (member or their provider) during a year?
5. What is your ability to measure and report for members across multiple carriers?
6. On the list of services below, what is the change in utilization for your business, comparing utilization for the year prior to the implementation of your services and the year after your services were implemented?

   - Primary care visits per 1,000
   - Preventive care services per 1,000
   - Specialist visits per 1,000
   - Outpatient diagnostics per 1,000
   - Outpatient surgery per 1,000
   - Inpatient admissions per 1,000
   - Average length of stay
   - Bed days per 1,000
   - Emergency room visits per 1,000

Those of you with long memories may note more than a passing similarity between this list and the questions we proposed in the Introduction.

Question 12: "How do you interface with Company-Sponsored Centers of Excellence (CSCOEs)?"

There are only two ways to save significant money without simply shifting costs to your employees—CSCOEs and care coordination. It would be nice if—given our discussion of silos—these weren't siloed programs. A real care coordination company should have experience in identifying people for CSCOEs very early, because the care coordinators should already know people who may qualify for the CSCOE program. People just aren't referred for transplants out of the blue. The care coordination company should be the one to bring the CSCOE program to people's attention in a timely manner.

Question 13: "How do you validly measure and guarantee outcomes?"

A benefit plan effective at increasing coordination of care will almost certainly demonstrate a track record of reducing healthcare cost trend over time. True care coordination achieves the triple aim of better care, better health, and lower cost. Therefore, in evaluating vendors, you should look at the following issues:

1. What is the total population healthcare claims cost trend for all members in all your clients over the past 36 months?
2. Do you compute savings using unit-based metrics or using pre-post for program participants?
3. What is the average patient satisfaction with your program for the last 12 months? Has there been any change in satisfaction levels in any month (plus or minus 10 percent from the average)? If so, please explain such deviation from the norm.
4. What questions are asked to measure satisfaction? (Please provide questions.)
5. What evidence can you provide of improved health status among your membership?
6. Are you financially backed as a Gold Standard vendor for the validity of your guaranteed cost reduction by the Disease Management Purchasing Consortium or another third party?

A Few Closing Words

Although care coordination is a fast-growing field, you can see why more self-insured employers don't do it. It requires actual work, with vendors (canceling contracts and transitioning), carriers (carving out certain functions, preferably in your carrier contract itself), and employees (changing their card so that they call a single 800 number, and possibly even tweaking the benefits design so that they have more incentives to call that number and hence get assistance). Also, as you can tell from the recommended RFP questions, your consultants are likely unfamiliar with care coordination and haven't written RFPs for it. A typical consulting firm RFP, cut-and-pasted from a template, will look like a disease management/wellness RFP rather than be geared to the purpose of finding the best care coordination vendor.

The total administrative fee (carrier plus care coordination vendor) is also higher with care coordination, since a care coordination vendor is doing much more. But that doesn't mean it costs more. Remember that administrative costs are typically only 10 percent of a health plan cost. You should expect a true care coordination vendor to do a much better job of controlling the 90 percent factor—claims cost—and therefore your total costs may very well be lower. In fact, Quantum Health, the vendor identified as the initial developer of this care coordination model, will put 100 percent of its fee at risk, by agreeing to be paid as a percentage of actuarially verified claims savings. That means if a care coordination program works the way it should, your total plan costs including admin fees are actually lower.

And of course, you will actually be doing something. Rather than just pretending to show savings using some pre-post methodology or comparison to a fictitious trend, care coordination allows you to achieve actual savings. And we think that's what you want. Otherwise why buy this book?

Chapter **10**

Goofus Retains a Wellness Vendor, Gallant Implements Well-Being

Reading an early draft of this book, someone asked me, "Tom, surely there must be someone, somewhere in the wellness space who can think outside the box to create a win-win for our key stakeholders?"

To which I replied, "Well, I wouldn't have thought it was possible, but if you can squeeze that many clichés into a single sentence, then anything is possible."

I started my search with the premise that a solution had to do what I said was needed. In Chapter 3, I note that true health is driven by many things, not simply the absence of illness. It's total well-being, of which physical health is only a part. It's not just me saying this. The 1946 Charter of the World Health Organization stated: "Health is a state of complete physical, mental, and social well-being and not merely the absence of disease or infirmity." See? It's exactly what I said, only with more syllables.

The problem in this field can be analogized to the old *Bob Newhart Show*. Bob was feeling fluey one day and was describing his symptoms to the orthodontist, Jerry. Jerry listened carefully and replied thoughtfully: "Sounds like an impacted molar." And that's exactly what happens with wellness—most of the hundreds of wellness vendors come from the same background and, as a result, all view the biggest impediment to enhanced workplace performance as a failure to eat healthy foods, exercise, and so on.

One vendor, Healthways, is leading the industry's transition from wellness to well-being. But before describing them, a little background, so you can see what we're talking about here. Caution: I'm afraid I'm going to have to utilize social science, arithmetic, and even some notes here, so don't expect the facile pseudoscience that wellness vendors write. Improving performance is hard work, and hard work does not make for easy reading.

What Is Well-Being?

Each individual's well-being is the measure of the combination of the physical, social, career, financial, and community factors that have been shown to affect individuals' current and future health and performance. The cost of healthcare and the cost of poor performance comprise the two elements of what we call *health-related costs* and, as you will see, greater well-being correlates with lower health-related costs. Further, successful well-being improvement programs will impact both, and do so on an individual and population basis.[1,2,3,4,5]

As I'll show you below, well-being can be scored,[6,7] and that score can also be used to calculate the financial value of both changes in job performance and healthcare cost as you change benefits, workplace policies, culture, and the like, the direct impact of which on health-related cost aren't easily measured.[8] In a sense this is the Holy Grail. Using well-being scores as the basis for determining financial value allows for clearer attribution of changes in cost to the things an employer is doing to enhance its employees' well-being.[9] For that to be doable, you'd have to be convinced of three things:

1. Well-being, and changes in well-being, can be accurately measured.
2. Differences in well-being equate to differences in health-related costs and performance.
3. Well-being scores can be improved through well-designed, well-implemented, and well-operated intervention models.

Remember, I am skeptical of most wellness interventions, but well-being improvement isn't wellness. Well-being improvement is a long-term investment in the health and performance of your employees, your organization, and in some cases your community (see the sidebar). Accordingly, I think there is both a good argument and emerging good evidence for each of these claims, even though I don't believe that to be the case for an incentive-enhanced health risk assessment (HRA), coaching, and screening-type wellness program.[10]

Well-Being Can Be Accurately Measured

The definitive measure of well-being is the Gallup-Healthways Well-Being Index™ (WBI).[11] Begun in 2008 as a way to collect unique data on the well-being of the U.S. population, *including* the roughly 80 percent of the population that has little or no interaction with the traditional healthcare system each year—a critical requirement for the development of well-being improvement initiatives for the *entire* population, not "participants" or "high-risk people." To date, taken daily in a rigorous method that assures accurate representation of the nation's population, nearly 2 million surveys have been completed, resulting in the world's largest behavioral economics database. The WBI samples a nationally representative population each night to measure the aggregate well-being of the United States. Nationwide results are produced nightly and are reported monthly. Because of the volume of completed surveys, the WBI also reports results annually on states, congressional districts, and even some municipalities.

As you no doubt recall one of the major sources of invalidity in measurement is vendors' insistence on measuring only a subset of the population—usually active participants who had high risk factors to begin with, thus assuring both self-selection bias and downward regression to the mean that will automatically show improvement even without an intervention. (As a result of this study design, multiple vendors claim savings on people who don't change.) This is not biostatistics. A valid measurement encompasses the entire population or a representative sample thereof, whether they participate or not, and no matter what their risk factors are.

Some of you might say, yes, but people still have to be willing to be surveyed, and some people simply won't answer the phone. That's an issue if you're trying to predict absolutes, like who is going to win an election, but not relative changes, where the bias is similar in every poll, making changes in the WBI valid.

By design, the WBI was not intended for the measurement of individual well-being or development of well-being improvement plans for each individual. To address that need, Healthways developed the Well-Being Assessment™ (WBA), an individually completed survey that combines the elements of the WBI with a traditional health risk assessment, productivity data for your organization, and other available health information.

The WBA allows you to measure the well-being of each of your employees and develop individual well-being plans for them. It also allows for comparisons across your business units and locations, identifying work environment and culture or policy deficits that may be contributing to lower well-being and, therefore, higher health-related costs. (The "therefore" is always a question mark, but, as the following Caterpillar example shows, it helps that multiple sites belonging to the same company do themselves correlate this way.)

Both the WBI and the WBA are validated instruments. In fact, in published research conducted by Drs. James and Janice Prochaska at the University of Rhode Island, individual well-being scores have been shown to be a valid and reliable measure and are significantly associated with measures of overall health and behavioral risks.[12] Similarly, the Prochaskas' research team developed and validated a measure of well-being-related presenteeism, or on-the-job productivity loss.[13] The WBA also has the Disease Management Purchasing Consortium (DMPC) Gold Standard rating, which means that the DMPC financially guarantees validity of the instrument's measurement. As part of being a valid study design, the WBA comparisons include both participants and nonparticipants in both the study and WBI-based comparison groups.

Blue Zones: Ground Zero for Well-Being

"In Blue Zones, people don't try to live to 100. It happens to them," says National Geographic explorer Dan Buettner, who examined the longest-living and healthiest people on the planet. Buettner discovered health and longevity lessons that these well-being-rich communities, called "Blue Zones," share and sought to apply them to populations within the United States, delivered in conjunction with Healthways solutions and tools that improve well-being and reduce health-related costs.

California's Beach Cities (Hermosa Beach, Manhattan Beach, and Redondo Beach) enrolled local employers and school districts in a concerted effort to improve local health and well-being. Many employers took the steps suggested in this chapter, and the Beach Cities also added community-wide improvements—bicycle-friendliness, changes to 60 restaurant menus, smoking restrictions, walk-to-school initiatives—that, in combination, moved the needle on well-being. To date, more than 15,000 citizens have participated in one or more Blue Zones Project initiatives.

Using valid cross-sectional Gallup polling (as opposed to just asking participants how they did), the community's WBI increased three points, driven by double-digit reductions in smoking and obesity rates and similar increases in exercising and healthy eating. Though difficult to measure because we don't have access to claims information for the population, that three-point improvement should generate a statistically significant reduction in hospital and emergency room utilization.

"We fought hard to bring the Blue Zones Project to the Beach Cities because we believed this preventative, community-based model would advance our ability to appreciably improve the lives of the residents we serve," said Susan Burden, CEO of Beach Cities Health District. "Having worked in healthcare management for more than 25 years, it is not often you have the opportunity to address health issues before it is too late, but the Blue Zones Project is making that possible. We are thrilled to see our community transforming in such a sustainable way and look forward to working with our residents to continue the positive momentum."

Do Differences in Well-Being Equate to Differences in Health-Related Cost?

Before you and I can sign on to the well-being improvement value proposition, we need to know that well-being scores correlate with the drivers of health-related cost. Fortunately, there is an ever-increasing body of research that indicates that they do. I've already mentioned the early work in this area by the Prochaskas. Another early study conducted by a large regional health plan found that employees with high indicators of well-being had 20 percent lower direct healthcare costs than the average, while employees with lower scores had direct costs 50 percent higher than average.[14] This study is population-based and cross-sectional, the gold standard of population health measurement.

At Lincoln Industries, a supplier of products requiring high-performance metal finishing, comparisons of well-being scores of its national award-winning[15] comprehensive population health management program demonstrated that changes in well-being were not a function of just being located in a community where workers were healthier. In fact, during a common timeframe, Lincoln Industries employees scored 4.5 percent higher on the WBI than the nation and 8.7 percent higher than the surrounding community. In the study,[16] Lincoln Industry employees showed statistically significant higher scores in the areas of physical health, emotional health, health behaviors, and basic access compared to other workers in Lincoln and nearby Omaha, Nebraska. These higher well-being scores correlated with Lincoln's calculation of a 77 percent reduction in the rate of heart attacks, 34 percent less diabetes, 45 percent less tobacco use, and 34 percent less depression.[17]

"But what," you ask, "is the impact of all this good stuff on Lincoln's financials?" The answer: as compared to its industry average, much lower workers compensation expense and (according to its own internal measures, which our resident outcomes guru Al has not reviewed) 50 percent lower healthcare costs.

In the realm of performance correlation, Caterpillar Corporation compared well-being scores of its employees to its internally developed business performance measurement for each of its 25 business units. The findings revealed a high correlation between well-being scores and overall performance, particularly in the top and bottom well-being score quintiles. These quintiles were characterized by high or low scores, respectively, across all the measured factors of well-being, not just an exceptionally high or low score on any one or two factors.[18] It's worth noting that while all categories correlated with performance, the difference between the highest and lowest scores was much greater in Life Evaluation and Work Environment than in the four health-related categories, meaning that these two categories—addressed by well-being but not wellness—had the greatest correlation with performance in this particular population at Caterpillar. That is why well-being transcends health-related issues in its attempt to boost employee performance.

In an analysis of collected data for a Fortune 100 company, the Healthways Center for Health Research found clear evidence that the business impact of high well-being is also evident at the individual level. In this study,[19] individual well-being scores were ranked in five categories—high, med-high, medium, med-low, and low. Scores for employees in the lower well-being score category were compared to the scores for employees in the high score category and the event odds were calculated for seven adverse outcomes, including:

1. Low intent to stay at the company
2. Low self-rating of performance

3. Low supervisor rating
4. Any self-reported absence in past month
5. Any short-term disability days
6. Any ER visits in past year
7. High claims costs

This methodology was also used for analysis[20] of data from a Fortune 100 company, except that the comparison was made to the medium category, and produced similar results. Specifically, employees with lower-than-average well-being showed at least a 150 percent greater likelihood of experiencing the adverse events listed above. By contrast, those in the high well-being category had more than 12 percent lower odds.[21] Further, employees in the high well-being category were 40 percent less likely to have an emergency room visit in the next 12 months than those in the medium category. On average, a 10-point positive difference in well-being score was associated with 5 percent fewer unscheduled absences, 24 percent lower presenteeism, 5 percent higher reported job performance, and 6 percent more days of "best work" in the preceding 28-day period.

Further evidence of the relationships between well-being and performance has been provided by researchers from the Health Enhancement Research Organization, Brigham Young, and other collaborators, who published two studies that took a detailed look at how well-being relates to presenteeism. The first study[22] showed, across three employers, that multiple dimensions of well-being contributed to presenteeism, with workplace support for well-being as an important factor. Workers who reported less support for well-being in the workplace, based on ability to exercise during the work day, access to healthy foods, and workplace support for physical and emotional health improvement were nearly twice as likely to be in the lowest quintile of presenteeism as those who reported support for well-being improvement activities.

The second study[23] found that workers with higher scores with respect to work environment factors were more than 15 percent more likely to have high self-rated job performance and were at least 16 percent less likely to have been absent in the past month as compared with workers with lower scores. Health behaviors, including smoking, healthy diet, and exercise, also impacted performance. Specifically, workers who ate healthily the entire day were 25 percent more likely to have high job performance and 16 percent less likely to have an absence, while workers who exercised regularly were 15 percent more likely to have high job performance and 27 percent less likely to have an absence.

In a study[24] of medical and pharmacy claims for one population—a health plan's members and employees—in the 12-month period following a baseline well-being assessment, a clear relationship emerged between low well-being and higher hospitalization and emergency room utilization compared to those employees with higher well-being. Specifically, for each one-point positive difference in well-being, employees were 2.2 percent less likely to have an admission, 1.7 percent less likely to have an ER visit, and had a 1 percent lower likelihood of incurring *any* healthcare cost. For those who did incur healthcare costs, each one-point positive difference in well-being was associated with 1 percent lower cost.

Another study[25] verified that employers can achieve financial value in a single year by improving employee well-being. For the Fortune 100 company, employees who improved their well-being by one score category (of the five discussed previously) reaped significant benefits, particularly when compared to their counterparts with well-being that decreased over the same one-year period. Specifically, employees whose well-being increased had, on average, $318.30 lower health care costs, 0.6 fewer unscheduled absences, self-rated presenteeism that was 10 points lower, and intention to stay with the company that was 2.5 points higher. Statistical testing found that change in well-being was a significant predictor of change in all of these outcomes, controlling for demographic factors.

Thing is, those are all correlations. Impressive ones, perhaps, but just correlations. And you can't know which came first. What you'd really like to do is show not correlation but actual causality, and do it across a population: Can increasing average well-being scores reduce health spending and increase productivity?

Well-Being Scores Can Be Improved

As I write this, the availability of outcomes studies is limited, principally because well-being is an emerging market solution. However, the Healthways Center for Health Research has reported on two significant populations to which its Well-Being Improvement Solution has been delivered.[26,27] The first was the Fortune 100 company referred to previously. The second was a small pilot population of 780 individuals at a Fortune 50 company.

At the Fortune 50 company, well-being was improved across the entire population in the first six months by a statistically significant 2.9 points from the baseline average score of 71.0.[28] At the Fortune 100 company, well-being was improved in the first year by a statistically significant 1.9 points from a baseline average score of 74.3.[29]

Translation of these results, and the concomitant impacts on utilization and performance reported in the previous section, is currently underway. However, unlike wellness vendors, which often find ROIs before the ink is even dry on their contract, Healthways recognizes that the effects of a comprehensive well-being solution grow over time. This fact has important implications for solution design and makes the ability to create and sustain engagement a critical success factor. And "engagement" doesn't just mean completing an HRA or returning a health coach's phone calls.

Requirements of an Effective Well-Being Improvement Program

Recall how we've said that creating a culture of wellness is hard work? A high well-being score is reflective of a very positive culture involving 100 percent of your population, which means that new elements must be designed to sustainably engage the population that is neither sick nor exhibiting meaningful health risk . . . but have perhaps relationship, financial, or other issues preventing them from focusing on their job and performing at peak.

Hence, as compared to a simplistic wellness program where you might be given a pedometer and a nicotine patch, the number and type of experts to which individuals need to have access must include not just clinical staff and coaches, but also financial planners, relationship counselors, and community and workplace built environment specialists.

Similarly, as increasing numbers of individuals become more comfortable with emerging communication technologies, an effective program must be able to interact with each individual in the form, manner, and time frame he or she desires. To do so requires the capability to deliver interactions on the web, by e-mail, by text, face-to-face through community social groups, by landline or smart phone, live and by interactive voice response (IVR), all supported by a shared health record and a comprehensive, ever-changing well-being improvement plan.

There are approximately—just ballparking it here—zero suppliers of population health services that, on their own, encompass the expertise in all these disciplines and frankly, I would be suspicious if any of them said they did. In the development and deployment of its well-being improvement solution, Healthways has entered into academic partnerships with MIT, the University of Michigan, Johns Hopkins, and Pro-Change Behavior Systems at the University of Rhode Island. In addition to its 25-year strategic relationship with Gallup, it also has exclusive partnerships with Activate Networks,[30] and Blue Zones,[31] Technology partnerships include Hewlett-Packard for software engineering, infrastructure, and platform, and Roundarch Isobar for web portal architecture and design.

Rounding out the list are four wholly owned subsidiaries: MeYou Health, producer of award-winning social media interventions at the intersection of mobile technology, social network science, gaming, and well-being improvement; HealthHonors, owner of the Dynamic Intermittent Reinforcement incentives model developed at Harvard; Navvis & Company, leading advisors to health systems on strategy, leadership, and performance; and Ascentia Health Care Solutions, providing comprehensive physician-directed population health solutions built on outcomes-based processes, systems, and tools developed by physicians for physicians.

Whew!

But that's just the beginning of what you should be looking for in terms of capabilities from your population health management solution supplier. Obviously, you should also be looking for track record, believability of performance promises, capability and soundness of measurement methodologies, alignment of performance objectives, and evidence of ability to sustainably engage your population, since absent that capability, no ROI or savings promise will ever be realized. You certainly want to know what else you have to buy—equipment, supplies, and so on—in order to access their services. And remember, even if the entity from which you purchase your population health management services takes performance risk, your real objective is never to collect. Doing so only means that you've wasted valuable time while figuring out that what you bought doesn't work.

Lastly, you should be sure that the program design and outcomes measurement have the DMPC Gold Standard or some other third-party willing to do the same: attest to validity *and* put money behind a letter of validation.

Even if you find a supplier with all these capabilities, however, successfully launching and sustaining a well-being improvement initiative for your company is not a fire-and-forget exercise. Successful initiatives must be led from the top.[32] Desired behaviors need to be consistently and continuously modeled. Benefits plan designs need to align with program objectives. Your policies, culture, and built environment should make the healthy choices the easy choices. You are likely to face some significant internal pushback. Well-being improvement, and the benefits it can deliver, is not a tactic, not a box to check in this year's plan. It's a strategic commitment to the future financial success of your organization.

Action Steps

I have never interacted with an employer that didn't assert at some point that its most important asset was its people. I wonder, however, why their behavior with respect to routine maintenance of that asset is arguably less than that they provide for their equipment and facilities.

Unlike hard assets, people don't have to depreciate. Ideally, you want your employees to be as productive as possible for as long as possible. Most companies, however, enter into wellness programs for the primary purpose of reducing their healthcare costs, failing to recognize that reduced healthcare costs are a natural byproduct of programs that actually improve the health and productivity of their employees and their organization.

So now you can see how my advice to clean the restrooms more often fits into the big picture. Restrooms are part of the "built environment," and the built environment is one major factor impacting well-being, and well-being is, at least as far as I can tell, the best measure of a company's likely health and productivity performance.

It's not just about the restrooms, of course. That's just a small example of how actively supporting an environment of well-being improvement for 100 percent of your employees increases morale and performance—in particular, the number and tenure of high-performing employees. It's not just that health-related costs should decline, but also that the cultural and individual well-being improvement should boost your performance. Both improvements should combine into a sustainable enhancement in your profitability.

Part III

What Should You Do Next?

Chapter 11

Health Insurance Exchanges: Should You Stay or Should You Go?

Health insurance exchanges are emerging as the new mechanisms for buying health insurance. Not only are many states and the federal government rushing to set up public exchanges as required by healthcare reform; numerous vendors are also establishing and operating private exchanges as a new way of transacting health insurance.

While the law restricts public exchanges to selling only to individuals and small employers (up to 100 employees for now, with the ability to expand to larger employers in the future), private exchanges have no such restrictions. As a result, they're targeting individuals and employers of every size, with the belief that employers and individuals will increasingly buy health insurance (and, as we'll see, other benefits) through these new marketplaces. Consulting firms, technology companies, services vendors, and start-ups are setting up private exchanges, attracting venture capital and other investors. Public exchanges need to be ready to sell health insurance starting October 2013, so the race is on to attract individuals and employers into them and to transform the process of purchasing health insurance.

This chapter offers an assessment of today's exchanges, a perspective on what exchanges should be doing in the future, and implications for employers in every size range. And speaking of implications, two sets of companies don't even have to read this chapter. The implications for them are already clear. If your workforce is old and unhealthy, what's stopping you from adopting this new approach? Go to the exchange and have your healthcare costs become someone else's problem. If your workforce is the opposite, stick with self-insurance. Everyone else—read the chapter.

Exchanges: The Basics

Exchanges are essentially insurance marketplaces that offer preselected plans and carriers. There are two types of exchanges: public (or state) and private. Though private exchanges, unlike state exchanges, are not a part of the Affordable Care Act, their customers and suppliers need to comply with the law's requirements. And whereas state exchanges currently offer only health and dental insurance, most private ones are establishing so-called "benefit exchanges" that also sell disability, life, and other insurance products. Additionally, most private exchanges take advantage of consumer familiarity with online shopping sites by including features like shopping carts, check-outs, and recommendation engines that suggest products individuals should buy based on their particular profiles.

You can now provide health insurance to your employees through one of the many private exchanges—or, if you are an eligible employer, through your state exchange. Healthcare reform imposes a penalty on organizations with more than 50 full-time employees that don't provide a minimum level of health insurance coverage deemed "affordable" using criteria laid out in the Affordable Care Act (ACA). Therefore, you need to determine the best way to offer insurance, whether it's through exchanges, full insurance, self-insurance, or exchanges for some classes of employees only.

I'll start with a quick primer on current and future exchanges, and then offer suggestions on what might be right for you depending on your company's size and other characteristics. I am fortunate to know one of the field's leading experts, Sanjiv Luthra, who has offered comments based on his 12 years of experience in setting up and operating exchanges.

Public Exchanges

Public exchanges are required to provide standardized plans (gold, silver, bronze, and so on) across multiple health plans, and to facilitate comparisons (though currently HHS is looking at delaying mandating the "multiple health plan" requirement to 2015). Since participating health plans have the potential to gain new membership at low marketing costs, the hope is that some of these participating health plans will price aggressively. Another hope is that the availability of bronze plans will lead many people to choose products that are relatively less expensive.

Public health exchanges will be most successful in attracting individuals below 400 percent of the federal poverty level who thus qualify for government subsidies and may attract others, but private exchanges are designed specifically to attract those others.

Private Exchanges

As mentioned earlier, private exchanges are not mandated by health-care reform law. However, many already exist, with more being developed. And unlike public exchanges—which only offer health insurance products (for now)—most private exchanges offer a wide spectrum of products, including vision, life, disability, and products like home, auto, and pet insurance as well as identity theft protection and legal services. Within health and dental, some private exchanges offer a choice of health plans with multiple designs, while others include multiple plan designs from only one health plan.

For employers, private exchanges offer simplicity and lower administrative cost. Think of all the vendors you now need to administer your benefit: analytics, network design, disease management, and so on. Now imagine others who are experts doing this work and reporting to someone else. You see only the finished product, available on these exchanges. And if they slip up, it doesn't affect your economics, which are driven by price, not the underlying cost. Using private exchanges also prevents employers from having to figure out what benefits and coverages they should offer their employees. (Whether this exercise is a chore or a strategy today depends on how well you do it, of course.) Employees benefit, because private exchanges address the problems of limited product choice and product understanding by offering more choices and explaining them better. That is, after all, their job.

Similar to public exchanges, purveyors of private exchanges are hoping that some carriers will price at least some of their products more aggressively due to exchanges being a central, presumably efficient, market. However, according to Luthra, selling health insurance products through a private exchange channel does not change the underlying health insurance product's cost:

> *Private exchanges are addressing the size of the benefit rather than the overutilization of healthcare services this book describes. They are doing so through three strategies—moving employers to defined contributions; establishing multiple health insurance products; and rebating commissions from non-health-insurance products. The idea is that if you give employees a fixed budget and a low-cost health option, many will migrate to that option. And, by the way, give them access to other products they buy today anyway like auto,*

home, and pet insurance at very competitive prices with no middle-man, and they will be happy. What's missing in the exchanges equation is anything that reduces healthcare utilization.

"Defined contribution" means giving your employees a fixed amount of money to purchase benefits. Offered by itself, this approach does not directly affect the underlying cost of providing insurance. Rather, it encourages people to buy less of it, by making them pay dollar-for-dollar extra for fancier plans.

Benefit exchange developers are hoping that including additional benefit products in their marketplace—and making it easier for employees to pay for them on an ongoing basis—will persuade many more employees to buy these products on their own. Unlike the situation with health insurance, brokers/exchange developers are legally allowed to rebate commissions from these additional products back to employers, thus possibly subsidizing an employer's cost of health benefits.

This seems like quite an indirect way to rebate a small share of commissions, but it's the only way. Due to some very impressive lobbying, the brokerage commissions for the core health insurance product remain sacrosanct, even though the broker's role might seem redundant if there is a central market. Basically, if you use a broker and an exchange, you are indirectly paying for two middlepeople—even if you don't see either brokerage fee directly. But since your price isn't affected by all this extra overhead, you might as well continue to use brokers until somebody in Washington figures out that brokerage services cost money, and that people who want to use those services should pay for them rather than be subsidized by people who don't see value in them.

Future Exchanges

Exchanges today offer primarily the same products that exist in the market today. There are just more of them, and they're ideally better organized and with clearer explanations. As we've seen throughout this book, the products themselves tend to enable overutilization; they certainly don't discourage it.

Very different future exchange models may clearly and explicitly focus on driving cost of healthcare at the consumer level and link purchase to usage and ultimately to health insurance. As Luthra describes it:

Usage drives the cost of purchased health insurance, just as it drives your self-insurance costs today. Therefore, successful exchange models will need to have products whose features and prices are explicitly connected to healthcare utilization. Examples of such features include:

- ◆ *If you want a private room instead of a shared room during hospitalization, your cost is $X more.*
- ◆ *If you want to get your primary care physician on the weekend and evenings, you can . . . but your cost is $Y more.*
- ◆ *If you get all your lab work at (for example) LabCorp or Quest Diagnostics, you will save $Z.*
- ◆ *And if you have a three-way meeting or phone conference between your PCP, specialist, and yourself to decide on a treatment protocol, you will save $X.*

Along with more consumer focus, the other thing you'll see is gradual elimination of the aforementioned middleperson. Expect to see some serious counter-lobbying once exchanges get a foothold in this market. They have lower costs than brokers do, and would much prefer a volume-based pricing structure, including rebates, to a fixed statutory margin where they or their insurance supplier have to pay off the broker and build those payoffs into their prices. Further, exchanges like Walmart (which has announced its intention to enter this field) can probably tie in their pharmacies and clinics to create a truly low-cost integrated offering.

How Does This Affect You?

It depends at least in part on the size of your organization.

Small Employer (fewer than 50 employees)

As cited earlier, employers with fewer than 50 employees do not incur a financial penalty for failing to provide health insurance. You want to consider instead the business value in providing this benefit; if there is any, you can then determine whether public or private exchanges are the easiest way to do so.

If you have fewer than 25 employees, cover at least 50 percent of the cost of healthcare coverage for your workers, and pay average annual wages below $50,000, then you are eligible for tax credits. Since they're only available only through public state exchanges, stick with them.

If you have more than 25 full-time employees and don't qualify for these credits, you should consider both public and private exchanges. You can still decline to offer your employees any benefits without paying a penalty, unless, of course, you grow beyond 50 employees.

As a small employer, your rates for the same product will be the same in private and public exchanges. Your choice of products, however, may be very different.

Mid–Size Employer (between 50 and 500 employees)

Starting in 2014, businesses with 50 or more full-time workers that do not provide adequate or affordable health insurance (once again as defined by ACA) will pay a financial penalty if any benefit-eligible employees receive a subsidy toward buying their health insurance on public exchanges.

You can continue providing benefits through your current arrangements with brokers and health plans. You are not eligible for public exchanges, but you do have the option to go to private.

On paper, most private exchanges offer more comprehensive benefits and better value administration than what many of you provide today. However, implementing some of the recommendations in this book should reverse that. Another option is to offer one self-insured product yourself and a defined contribution for anyone who would like a different product. You could offer a high-deductible plan, but— contributing the same dollar subsidy—send people who want a gold-plated plan to a private exchange. Those folks are likely to expect and experience higher utilization than people selecting the self-insured high-deductible plan, so you should see an immediate financial benefit by not being at risk for them.

Luthra believes that many companies with 50 to 500 employees will find current models of private exchanges most attractive:

Most [companies of this size] don't have the resources to manage benefit selection, procurement and ongoing administration. In order to avoid penalties, they now need to ensure that their health insurance coverage is both reasonable and affordable—and private exchanges have prepackaged and preassembled benefit products that meet reform's product coverage guidelines. They also work with these companies to determine the right employer contribution that would meet the affordability requirement.

Mid-Size Employer (between 500 and 5,000 employees)

Because you have more resources and financial capabilities than companies with 50 to 500 employees, you can continue self-insuring—adding some of the recommendations in this book.

However, some employers with 500 to 5,000 employees do need to look at private exchanges, as Luthra explains:

Some larger mid-size companies are getting pressure from their management to justify their benefits procurement and management efforts, efforts that often consume 15 percent of the healthcare dollar. These companies should determine if the more efficient administration through the exchange does, in fact, reduce their total cost of coverage, including administration. They can still cobrand their benefits with the exchange developers without being bogged down with the administrative details about what to provide and how to administer.

Large Employer (more than 5,000 employees)

Most large companies have the resources to provide comprehensive benefits, though as we've seen in this book, they often don't deploy those resources well. Attractive benefits design can create strong employee retention and loyalty. In addition, at this size, self-insurance should confer a significant cost advantage compared to fully insured offerings on the exchange, which will suffer from adverse selection. Large companies are also active in employee engagement programs that rarely actually save money but because they always look like they do, large companies are reluctant to give them up.

So what certain advantage do exchanges offer you as a large company? A solution for part-time employees, suggests Luthra: "The non-benefit-eligible part-time workforce is growing as employers take advantage of the 30-hour cutoff point. Even with little or no employer contribution, private exchanges offer a great vehicle for these employers to provide access to health benefits."

"Should I Stay or Should I Go?"

Throughout *Cracking Health Costs*, I have usually been quite adamant about one view or another. And in the following two scenarios, I am. To repeat what I said earlier in this chapter (they say things need to be said three times in order to sink in, so read this paragraph twice):

1. For those "old economy" companies that have high claims costs, the answer may already be clear: let someone else insure your employees. Based on your own adverse selection, the arithmetic should reveal that it is much less expensive to make them someone else's problem.
2. Likewise, the Googles of the world should self-insure. There's no sense in having your young and healthy workforce become a windfall for an insurance company.

The answer is more nuanced for everyone in between, and because there are so many unknowns, we can offer two starkly contrasting views. You'll need to decide which fits you better.

The first is the more conventional: unless you have fewer than 500 employees, chill. The exchanges will always be there, and—like almost any innovation—should improve over time. Meanwhile, you have the opportunity to maintain or expand your self-insured cost advantage over any fully insured product by implementing the recommendations in this book. And you maintain control of your benefits, as well.

The second is a bit more dramatic. Unless your benefits consultants offer exchanges (as many will be doing in order to collect added fees), they will try to convince you to remain self-insured, to keep their own train smothered in your gravy. But, in addition to being sold add-on products of no value as described in this book, have you ever really added up the hidden costs of self-administration? The paralysis in HR and lost workplace productivity during open-enrollment period? The phones ringing off the hook in January when some of the providers and coverages change? The rushes to the doctor and pharmacy to beat benefits design changes? The headaches of COBRA? The logistics of distributed work forces?

Wherever I worked, managers consistently reported that half the complaints they heard when they toured facilities and talked directly to employees were about the health benefits. And this doesn't even begin to cover the blame employers incur every time the cost of health insurance rises or an insurer denies a referral or botches a claim.

I realize that, as Yogi Berra said, "It's hard to make predictions, especially about the future," but here's mine: by 2016 you'll be amazed at the number of large companies that move to the exchanges or even (in the case of low-wage companies with high turnover) opt out of the system altogether and simply pay the penalty. If that happens, it may be, in a perverse way, because *Cracking Health Costs* has done its job. It's shown you that there is so much broken in your health benefit, so many self-interested providers, vendors, and consultants feeding at your trough, and so much angst among your employees, that it might simply be a better idea to focus on your base business—and let the health insurers handle the health insurance.

Notes

Chapter 3

1. Larry Chapman, "Meta-Evaluation of Worksite Health Promotion Economic Return Studies," *American Journal of Health Promotion* (March/April 2012), www.chapmaninstitute.net/articles/05_TAHP_26_4_Meta_Evaluation_2012.pdf. doi:10.4278/ajhp.26.4.tahp.
2. Katherine Baicker, David Cutler, and Zirui Song, "Workplace Wellness Programs Can Generate Savings," *Health Affairs* 29, no. 2 (2010): 304–311.
3. Al Lewis and Vik Khanna, "Is It Time to Re-Examine Workplace Wellness 'Get Well Quick' Schemes?" Healthaffairs.com (January 16, 2013), http://healthaffairs.org/blog/2013/01/16/is-it-time-to-re-examine-workplace-wellness-get-well-quick-schemes/.

Chapter 8

1. www.altarum.org/files/imce/Steering%20Employees%20Safer%20Care_LeapFrog_WhitePaper_Final.pdf.
2. http://oig.hhs.gov/oei/reports/oei-06-09-00090.pdf.
3. http://resources.iom.edu/widgets/vsrt/healthcare-waste.html.

Chapter 10

1. P. L. Harrison et al., "Evaluation of the Relationship between Individual Well-Being and Future Health Care Utilization and Cost," *Population Health Management* 15, no. 6 (December 2012): 325–330.

2. Y. Shi et al., "Classification of Individual Well-Being Scores for the Determination of Adverse Health and Productivity Outcomes in Employee Populations," *Population Health Management* 16, no. 2 (2013): 90–98.

3. L. E. Sears et al., "Overall Well-Being as a Predictor of Healthcare, Productivity, and Retention Outcomes in a Large Employer," *Population Health Management* (March 12, 2013).

4. W. Gandy et al., "Well-Being and Employee Health—How Employees' Well-Being Scores Interact with Demographic Factors to Influence Risk of Hospitalization or an Emergency Room Visit," *Population Health Management*, (April 5, 2013).

5. Y. Shi et al., "The Association between Modifiable Well-Being Risks and Productivity: A Longitudinal Study in a Pooled Sample," *Journal of Occupational and Environmental Medicine* 55, no. 4 (2013): 353–364.

6. Sears et al., "Overall Well-Being as a Predictor."

7. Gandy et al., "Well-Being and Employee Health."

8. Shi et al., "The Association between Modifiable Well-Being Risks and Productivity."

9. K. E. Evers et al., "Development of an Individual Well-Being Scores Assessment," *Psychology of Well-Being: Theory, Research and Practice* 2, no. 2 (2012).

10. Gallup-Healthways Well-Being™ Index: Methodology Report for Indexes, 2009. Available at www.well-beingindex.com/methodology.asp.

11. www.well-beingindex.com.

12. Evers et al., "Development of an Individual Well-Being Scores Assessment."

13. J. O. Prochaska et al., "The Well-being Assessment for Productivity: A Well-being Approach to Presenteeism," *Journal of Occupational and Environmental Medicine* 53, no. 7 (2011): 735–742.

14. Healthways Center for Health Research analysis, 2008.

15. Innovation in Prevention Award, U.S. Department of Health and Human Services; C. Everett Koop National Health Award four-time winner, 25 Best Small to Medium Companies to Work for in America Award.

16. R. M. Merrill et al., "Evaluation of a Best-Practice Worksite Wellness Program in a Small-Employer Setting Using Selected Well-Being Indices," *Journal of Occupational and Environmental Medicine* 53, no. 4 (April 2011): 448–454.

17. Integrated Benefits Institute, 2011. "Workforce Health and Productivity: How Employers Measure, Benchmark and Use Productivity Outcomes."

18. Ibid.

19. Shi et al., "Classification of Individual Well-Being Scores."

20. Proprietary Customer Analysis, Center for Health Research, 2012.

21. Alternative representation of data published in Shi et al., "Classification of Individual Well-Being Scores."

22. R. M. Merrill et al., "Presenteeism According to Healthy Behaviors, Physical Health, and Work Environment," *Population Health Management* 15, no. 5 (October 2012): 293–301.

23. R. M. Merrill et al., "Self-Rated Job Performance and Absenteeism According to Employee Engagement, Health Behaviors, and Physical Health," *Journal of Occupational and Environmental Medicine* 55, no. 1 (January 2013): 10–18.

24. Harrison et al., "Evaluation of the Relationship."

25. Sears et al., "Overall Well-Being as a Predictor."

26. Ibid.

27. Manuscript in preparation (Fortune 50 company).

28. Ibid.

29. Sears et al., "Overall Well-Being as a Predictor."

30. Social networks analytics company founded in the social science research of Nicholas Christakis of Harvard, James Fowler of UCSD, and Rob Cross of the University of Virginia.

31. Community-based environment well-being improvement solutions.

32. M. S. Taitel et al., "Incentives and Other Factors Associated with Employee Participation in Health Risk Assessments," *Journal of Occupational and Environmental Medicine* 50, no. 8 (2008): 863–872.

Bibliography

M uch of what is recommended in the last couple of hundred pages recommends that you spend less—and shows you how to spend less—than you are spending now. This is not because Al and I are cheapskates. It's not a political statement, either. Quite the contrary. *Cracking Health Costs* is one of the few apolitical books on the topic of health insurance. (Look at Amazon's rather oxymoronically titled "list of health insurance best sellers." In addition to stultifyingly dull coding manuals, Al's book and hopefully *Cracking Health Costs*, all these books have titles like *How American Healthcare Killed My Father* and *Uninsured in America: Life and Death in the Land of Opportunity*. There should be a separate Amazon health insurance book category for right- and left-wing polemics, though those two are both excellent books on their merits.)

Therefore, our theme of generally spending less is not our way of circumventing the Affordable Care Act, but rather a reflection of our sincere and, more important, data-driven belief that far more insured people have been harmed by too much healthcare than too little. I recommend *Overdiagnosed* by Dr. Gilbert Welch and *Overtreated* by Shannon Brownlee as two meticulously researched books that, well, you can tell from the titles what the themes are. *How We Do Harm: A Doctor Breaks Ranks about Being Sick in America* by Dr. Otis Brawley is more of a first-person medical narrative but might be an easier read. The real-life vignettes in *How We Do Harm* bring to life the two more data-intensive books.

An outstanding series of books by Dr. Nortin Hadler is profoundly enlightening, starting with *The Last Well Person: How to Stay Well Despite the Health-Care System*. If you read that book, your view of healthcare in America will never be the same.

You'll be shocked—*shocked*—to hear that the final recommendation along these lines is *Why Nobody Believes the Numbers* by Al Lewis, a hilarious smackdown of vendors, consultants, and actuaries who forgot one of the cardinal rules of arithmetic, namely that numbers aren't designed to decorate pages.

In addition, if you thought the third-party commentary in *Cracking Health Costs* was insightful, you might enjoy the books by the commentators themselves. Paul Levy's *Goal Play!* draws on anecdotes from his experience as an executive leader and youth soccer coach to offer insights from sports, healthcare, business, and government to help leaders get better outcomes. *YOU Are the CEO of Your Health* by Cyndy Nayer observes that health is your greatest asset, and this book provides the map to manage your asset for the best performance, just as a CEO manages a successful company.

Acknowledgments

To paraphrase the immortal words of the great philosopher Yogi Berra, Al and I would like to thank everyone who made this book necessary. Those would be the wellness vendors, carriers, consultants, pharmacy benefit managers, and provider organizations that have been making huge profits from their corporate customers for years or (in the case of some benefits consultants) decades, with shockingly little regard for the health of those customers' employees or the fact that healthcare expenses keep rising. They have selflessly provided us with an abundance of material.

Transitioning from good material to a book isn't easy—it requires a lot of support from family and friends. Or at least that's the cliché. In fact, writing *Cracking Health Costs* required almost no support from anybody. You're always reading in acknowledgments how family and friends encouraged the project, helped the author overcome writer's block, persuaded the author not to abandon the book when it wasn't going well, pored over the manuscript making brilliant editorial suggestions, turned off the engine during the author's suicide attempt, and so on.

Well, our families have lives, and people who read *Cracking Health Costs* won't be surprised to learn we don't have any friends. Fortunately, with editors like Adrianna Johnson, Christine Moore, and Linda Indig, and a publisher like John Wiley & Sons, we don't need many. Everyone at Wiley was terrific.

There are some people who really do need acknowledging. All of them are acknowledged in the book itself as experts who have contributed their time and knowledge to provide best-of-breed insights. But I would like to offer a special shout-out to Leah Binder, without whom this book would not exist. She introduced us. Our skills and philosophies dovetailed so well, and our telephone connections were so clear, that we've managed to complete this book without ever having met in person. Thanks to Leah, long distance truly is the next-best thing to being there.

Speaking of acknowledging my co-author Al Lewis, you can blame him for most of the too-clever-by-half lines in this book, like "it's time for the wellness industry to admit to doping" and "no employee has ever complained to management that the restrooms are too clean." (Also the second and third paragraphs of these very same acknowledgments, which he cribbed from his previous book, on the theory that nobody reads the Acknowledgments anyway.)

About the Authors

Tom Emerick

Tom Emerick is a consultant, blogger (www.crackinghealthcosts.com), and speaker on the topic of overutilization and overtreatment, along with other topics in health benefits and economics. He is President of Emerick Consulting and chief strategy officer with Laurus Strategies, a Chicago-based consulting firm. His specialty had been advising benefits administrators on how to protect their employees and covered dependents from medical care that is either poor quality or unethical, or both.

Prior to his consulting career, Tom was vice president, global benefit design, for Walmart, where he pioneered the domestic "medical travel" program that ultimately became the Company-Sponsored Centers of Excellence program described in these pages. Prior to Walmart, Tom had similar positions with Burger King Corporation, British Petroleum, and American Fidelity Assurance Company.

In 2009, Tom was named by Healthspottr as one of the top 100 innovators in healthcare in the United States for his work on medical ethics. In 2013, a Forbes.com article by Leah Binder named Tom one of 13 "Unsung Heroes Changing Health Care Forever" for his work both in understanding the drivers of overutilization and in recognizing and rewarding high-quality providers.

Tom has served on the boards of many employer coalitions and associations, including the National Business Group on Health, and the U.S. Chamber of Commerce Benefit Committee.

In demand as a speaker for benefits and healthcare conferences such as the internationally known World Health Care Congress, Tom's topics include strategic health plan design, global health care challenges, healthcare economics, and evidence-based medicine.

Al Lewis

Search on the phrase "invented disease management" and you will find Al Lewis. Mr. Lewis was also founder and first president of the Disease Management Association of America, now the Care Continuum Alliance. His Critical Outcomes Report Analysis certification, the only credential specifically devoted to population health management outcomes analysis, has been earned by about 200 professionals, and he has been cited as the leading care management outcomes guru in the country by many people, including some he's never even slept with.

He provides procurement and outcomes consulting to health plans through www.dismgmt.com, the Disease Management Purchasing Consortium, and (in conjunction with the Institute for Health and Productivity Management) to employer human resource departments through www.hchc-consortium.com, the Health Care and Human Capital Consortium. Having earned a JD from Harvard Law School, he also provides forensic consulting to companies who've noticed that their vendors and consultants have made a big enough mess of things that they should return their fees, but asking them nicely didn't work.

His previous book, named on Forbes.com as the 2012 Healthcare Book of the Year, is *Why Nobody Believes the Numbers*. *Why Nobody Believes* introduced one of the themes of *Cracking Health Costs*, which is that both the wellness industry and the benefits consulting industry were absent the day the fifth-grade teacher covered arithmetic. (Al places the blame for those industries' cluelessness directly on the backs of our nation's truant officers.) Call him an "outcomes Nazi," but he insists that vendors and consultants present only ROIs that meet his exacting standard, which is actually being achievable right here on this very planet.

He speaks widely—basically in front of any audience that will pay his fee, buy some books, and spring for upgrading him to the "even more legroom" seats—and has written for and been interviewed in all sorts of major national media. He won't bore you with the list and in any event he's hoping the list will be longer by the time you read this, so he suggests Googling. And the good news is you can Google him until you're blue in the face and you won't find any priors.